A Special Need for INCLUSION

Children with Disabilities, their Families and Everyday Life

JULIA WIDDOWS

The Children's Society
MAKING LIVES WORTH LIVING
A VOLUNTARY SOCIETY OF THE CHURCH OF ENGLAND
AND THE CHURCH IN WALES

First published in 1997

The Children's Society
Edward Rudolf House
Margery Street
London WC1X 0JL

A catalogue record of this book is available from
The British Library.

ISBN 1 899783 06 7

Edited by Christopher Pick

Cover photograph: David Tothill – Photofusion

Contents

Acknowledgements

The research team consisted of Jackie Burgess, Jenny Clench and Julia Widdows.

We would like to thank all the young people and the parents who took part in this research and made it possible. We would also like to thank our team of interviewers, the members of Carousel who carried out the group work, the teachers and care staff who made the group work possible, and our research steering group for their practical help and general support. We very much valued the interest and enthusiasm of everyone involved.

CHAPTER *1*

Introduction

This report seeks to explore many different aspects of the everyday family life of parents of children with disabilities, through their own experiences and comments. As far as possible, the parents have been left to speak for themselves. In addition, the views of teenagers with disabilities are given. A short concluding chapter examines the implications for policy and practice of the views and experiences reported in the body of the text.

OVERVIEW AND LITERATURE REVIEW

In providing an in-depth view of the everyday lives of families with disabled children, wherever possible using the words of those most closely involved, this study helps to fill a gap in the existing literature. By focusing on the quality of the everyday experience, it provides a contrast with other recent publications. These approach the topic either from the point of view of professional practitioners, whether in education or social work, or examine wider socio-economic issues. A broadly similar study is *Disabled in Britain: Behind Closed Doors* (Lamb and Layzell, 1995), which reports the experience of carers of all ages. *Expert Opinions* (Beresford, 1995) analyses the specific practical needs of parents caring for children with severe disabilities. *Disabled in Britain: A World Apart* (Lamb and Layzell, 1994) examines the experience of adults with disabilities. *Unequal Opportunities* (Bennett and Abrahams, 1994) is a wide-ranging investigation of the impact of new legislation and financial changes on the quality of life and financial circumstances of children with disabilities and their families. *Living in the Real World* (Goodey, 1991) reports, with a minimum of editorial comment, the experiences and feelings of parents of Down's Syndrome children. Perhaps closest of all to the present study is *Positively Parents*

(Beresford, 1994), which examines how parents care for severely disabled children.

All parents would recognise that being a parent can be a demanding and difficult job at times, as well as a joyful one. Parents of children with disabilities are no exception. However, even in the most testing moments, parents of non-disabled children can always look forwards – for them childhood is an evolving process and they know that in time their children will develop and grow towards independence. This is not the case with many parents of children with disabilities, who have to come to terms with the fact that their child may always be dependent: not for them the relief from the tasks of caring and the pleasure of watching their children grow increasingly independent and self-reliant. Hales (1996) describes the sense of loss parents experience as they discover that their expectations for their child will have to be modified. Lamb and Layzell (1995) write:

> Caring for a disabled child differs from caring for a non-disabled child because parents are rarely able to look forward to the future in the same way; not necessarily because of their child's disability per se but because disabled people have fewer opportunities to lead independent lives.

RESPITE CARE

Respite care allows parents a much-needed break from the tasks of caring and, perhaps of equal importance, extends the horizons and experiences of children with disabilities. *They Keep Going Away* (Oswin, 1984 and 1991), based on research undertaken in the late 1970s and early 1980s, was critical of the quality of many residential care services for children with disabilities. However, for many of the parents reported in the present book (see Chapter 3) reasonably frequent regular respite care (i.e. a few hours or a single day on a weekly or fortnightly basis), provided either in the family home or in a local day centre, is of great importance, allowing them time to live their own lives, catch up with household chores and devote time to their other children. *Sharing the Caring* (Geall and Host, 1991), which surveys the provision and quality of respite care services in the UK, reinforces this and emphasises the far-reaching impact that the physical and emotional demands of caring for children with disabilities can have on the disabled child's brothers and sisters.

Respite care also provides positive support for the parent–child relationship. After a period of respite care, parents look forward to seeing their child again. However, support services for the parent must suit or meet the child's needs; if their child does not enjoy or benefit from the respite care, parents will be reluctant to use the service (Beresford, 1994, 1995).

THE FAMILY UNIT

A young child with disabilities is very likely to be part of a young family, but all too often specialist services fail to recognise this and fail to plan for the needs of the family as a whole (Chapter 3). As Hornby (1994) observes:

> *Many practitioners in the disability field consider themselves to be working with individual clients quite independently of their families and believe that this work will only affect the children or adults directly involved. However, ... intervention with a person with a disability will have an impact on the whole family to which that person belongs.*

Newson and Davies (1994) comment that:

> *In many ways the professional attitudes on disability have mirrored the family predicament, in that the need to focus clearly on the disabled child, in order to compensate for his difficulties as fully as possible, has tended to make the other children invisible.*

Parents find themselves climbing aboard a special needs 'merry-go-round' – a whole world of therapeutic input and specialist expertise devoted to their child (Chapter 3). However, parents have to orchestrate the provision. This can impose great strains on the family and prevent their child living an 'ordinary' childhood. There is a danger that both child and parents will become primarily 'patients', subjects of intervention, rather than individual people with their lives to lead. John Swain writes in *Disabling Barriers – Enabling Environments* (Swain *et al.*, 1993) of a school for young disabled people:

> *The system ... [creates] dependency in that young people [are]*

passed from the hands of one professional to another, pressurised by the demands of each professional discipline, and [have] their 'needs' determined by others. Young people [are] caught up in a whirlwind of activity with, to quote a social worker, 'the teachers and the physios and the medics arguing out who has this square inch of this kid's time'.

The parents interviewed for this study would say much the same thing.

Parents do their best to minimise the impact on siblings of having a brother or sister with disabilities (Chapter 3). Don and Marilyn Weinhouse (1994) write that:

The strain of having a sibling with exceptional needs can be particularly hard on a child. Parents who watch, listen and are sensitive to behavioural and emotional changes in themselves and their family members, and take action when those changes are not in a desirable direction, are doing the most important things they can to minimise the negative effects of the challenges inherent in raising a child with exceptional needs.

Young siblings do not generally carry out any caring tasks that could be described as extraordinary for a child of that age. Rather, they do what any child would want to do to help a brother or sister who is not fully able-bodied, or who is unwell (Beresford, 1994). However, siblings often feel isolated, and also upset and angry because their brother or sister needs extra attention. The kinds of outings that many children take for granted are liable to be less frequent when there is a child with special needs in the family (Atkinson and Crawforth, 1995). However, as this study clearly shows, the experience can also be a positive one, and can develop and reinforce qualities of tolerance and understanding. Hornby (1994) writes:

Siblings of children with disabilities tend to be more insightful and tolerant of others' difficulties, to be more certain of their goals in life, to demonstrate greater social competence, and to develop a maturity beyond their years.

THE OUTSIDE WORLD

Positive relationships with the outside world – through friends and the wider family, leisure activities, outings and holidays (Chapter 4) – are as important for a child with disabilities as for parents and siblings. Each family is made up of interlocking social relationships, within the family itself and also with wider social groups – extended family, friends, work colleagues, cultural groups (Dale, 1996). If these are restricted, both through a disability and through the need to spend time on special medical and educational provision, a child's social education – which cultivates her or his ability to interact with the world – can be limited. Don and Marilyn Weinhouse (1994) comment that special provision pulls children away from the mainstream of childhood:

Special programs begin replacing day care and preschool; therapies become the focus instead of play, dance, swimming, and other more typical activities; and more and more time is spent learning and socializing with other 'exceptional' children and less time with kids who are more 'typical'.

Parents and professionals must seek an appropriate balance between meeting the exceptional needs of a child and including that child in activities and groups with all types of children.

Integrated activities can stimulate and encourage a child with disabilities and help her or him to take a place in the able-bodied world. However, by the same token, participation can be discouraging if it is notional – if the organisers of activities are not prepared to adapt their activities to match the abilities of children with disabilities. Accepting attitudes, on the part of both adults and children, are equally important. As *Unequal Opportunities* (1994) makes clear, children with disabilities want to take part in the same sort of activities as other children and gain more independence from their parents as they get older.

However, the design of buildings, both public and private, and above all, the attitudes of other people – professionals, other children and society as a whole – prevent them from doing so. Achieving the laudable objective of 'integration' is perhaps more multi-faceted and complex an operation than is often recognised; and integration without true acceptance and understanding from their peers and the public is going to seem a very hollow exercise to children such as these. As the parents in this report attest, integration can all too often mean participation on able-bodied terms.

The support of extended family – grandparents, brothers and sisters – and a wider social network of friends, can make all the difference to the first few years of parenting (Chapter 5). Yet support is not always forthcoming to parents of a child with disabilities. Hornby (1994) reports that:

Generally grandparents ... provide minimal support for the families caring for their disabled grandchildren.

However, Beresford (1994) states that:

On the whole it [is] the grandparents who [are] the source of support from within the extended family.

Close friends are often other parents of children with disabilities. They can share experiences and provide practical support, advice and, above all, understanding. Other friends, particularly with non-disabled children of the same age, can fade away, especially as the children grow older and their differences become more marked. Hales (1996) reports:

Parents of a learning disabled child will often feel that they are treated differently from other new parents as people often don't know what to say and this can lead to the family being cut off from much social contact. Rebecca felt that her friends were embarrassed when their children started to develop so much more quickly and this meant that she felt out of place on the trips to the park and other occasions when the mothers and babies got together.

As a child with disabilities grows, public attitudes (Chapter 5) become much more important to parents and to children themselves. Parents tire of having to explain about their children and of confronting public indifference, at times hostility. The child's or young person's acceptance of their own disability is crucial if self-esteem is to develop: hence the importance of mixing with non-disabled peers. Appleton (1995) writes:

Teenagers with disabilities, like most teenagers, want to establish themselves in a variety of community leisure facilities ... Leisure activities with peers carry challenges which require the young person to develop new social, cognitive, and physical skills.

*Feeling socially accepted in a peer group is just as important for
self-esteem in teenagers, as having close friendships.*

RESEARCH METHODOLOGY

The research was designed, directed and carried out by the Brighton
Portage Service on behalf of The Children's Society. Portage's way of
working – in partnership with parents, teaching children achievable
goals through small steps – shaped the design of the research. Portage
is used to fitting in with the needs and wishes of the family, and to
trusting the good sense, knowledge and instincts of parents. To obtain
a picture of the everyday lives of children with disabilities that
reflected their richness and variety, an interview schedule was
designed to prompt parents to tell interviewers as much or as little as
they wanted about their child's inclusion in various aspects of ordinary
living with a young family.

The research team was advised by a steering group consisting of heads
of two local special schools, the care services manager of a residential
unit for young people with disabilities, a disability consultant, a representative of Carousel (see page 9), the Portage Service's manager, a parent of
a disabled child involved in the research and a representative of the interviewing team with experience in research in health service settings.

The research itself was carried out with two discrete groups: parents
and young people.

PARENTS

The research was conducted between April and September 1994 in the
form of a tape-recorded interview lasting approximately one hour and
carried out at the parents' homes. It was felt that a set questionnaire
would limit answers to topics identified in advance by the research
team and would hinder families identifying their own issues, problems
and solutions. The interviews were therefore free-flowing, although
they were based on a schedule of core questions.

In order to make best use of the time available, parents were sent a
list of the topics in advance so that they could, if they wished, priori-
tise areas of importance or decide not to cover certain topics. As it
turned out, no parents prioritised a particular topic or actively chose to
leave any out.

The families invited to participate came from the following categories:

- those currently involved with the Portage Service (i.e. with children aged under 5);

- parents of past Portage families (i.e. with children aged 5 and over);

- parents of children in the nursery classes of two local special schools (i.e. with children aged under 5);

- two parents of the young people (aged 12 to 19) who participated in the school-based group work (see below).

In all, thirty-one interviews were held. Thirty-seven adults contributed. Twenty-three mothers, one father and one grandmother (a significant carer) gave individual interviews, while six couples were interviewed together. The total number of families was twenty-nine, one of which had two children with special needs.

The pattern of disabilities was as follows:

- six children had a physical disability (cerebral palsy, chronic juvenile arthritis, etc.) without any intellectual impairment;

- eighteen children had a learning disability (Down's Syndrome, autistic spectrum, no specific diagnosis, etc.);

- six children had multiple and profound disabilities (cerebral palsy, combination of disabilities, global delay with no specific diagnosis, etc.).

All the children involved had experienced significant developmental delay and could be expected to have some or all of their education in special schools or other provision. Most of the families lived in Brighton and Hove and the surrounding suburbs, a few in smaller towns such as Lewes and Newhaven, or in rural districts.

The research team (see above) trained the interviewers specially for the project, although some had previous interviewing experience. Most of the interviewers were past and current Portage Home Visitors, who were therefore familiar with local support services for families with a child with special needs, as well as with the local community. They were also used to working in the home with families with a child with disabilities and had developed good listening skills. This was very helpful in promoting free-flowing interviews.

YOUNG PEOPLE

Like all teenagers, young people with disabilities can be presumed to hold different opinions, and to have different experiences and hopes, from their parents. Indeed, their parents may not always be aware of their ideas and aspirations.

Interviews are not an appropriate method for collecting opinions from young people with significant disabilities. Instead, it was decided that group work, closely focused on a few of the topics covered in the interviews with parents, would allow data to be collected without exploiting the young people and help the young people concerned to think about the issues and put over their views. Carousel, a Brighton-based creative arts project for people of all ages with learning difficulties, was selected to provide a safe and stimulating environment in which the young people could enjoy expressing their views. Carousel had substantial experience in communicating with people with disabilities and had already established links with the three establishments involved.

Carousel worked with three separate groups of young people: two classes in different special schools (a school for pupils with severe learning difficulties and a school for pupils with physically disabling conditions); and one group in a residential setting for young people with severe physical or multiple disabilities. Each group was already established and the members knew one another well. Carousel ran two sessions with each group.

The research team briefed the Carousel workers, observed at least one session with each group and checked with the groups that the material selected from their work was acceptable.

Carousel used talking, writing and drawing to gather impressions of what it is like to be a disabled young person in a largely able-bodied world. Through working on ideas such as 'myself', 'my room', 'my journey to school', 'my holiday' and 'shopping', the young people focused purposefully, and voiced their views about the activities they preferred and their wishes for the future. All the work was related in a concrete way to the individuals involved, each of whom was helped by a facilitator to express ideas through words and pictures. It was not appropriate to cover the variety or depth of issues dealt with in the parent interviews, partly because of time constraints but largely because of the young people's disabilities. The facilitators worked hard to involve each young person and to check that what was recorded was indeed what they had wished to say; later feedback sessions were used as confirmation. The young people themselves worked extremely hard and were very involved with the whole group process.

All names have been changed in order to preserve anonymity. Reference to the age or disability of the child is included only when this sheds extra light on the quotation selected.

CHAPTER 2

The importance of inclusion

What is life like for a child or young person with disabilities? How, and how far, do they take part in all the normal, everyday things that children and young people do – from everyday visits to the park to special treats such as a meal out in a restaurant? How do they take their place in the social network that stretches through the immediate and extended family outwards to friends and the local community? How do they and their parents cope with the demands made by specialist therapeutic and educational services? How do parents organise family life, and how do they balance the sometimes conflicting needs of a disabled child and non-disabled brothers and sisters?

The research described in this book sets out to discover the answers to these and many similar questions. The aim is to capture, as directly as possible, the feelings, views and experiences of children with disabilities themselves and of their parents. It is the parents of children who are too young to voice their own opinions, or who lack the ability to do so, who are are best placed to know those children's interests and to speak on their behalf. Parents are, after all, the people most expert in their own child.

The desire of children with disabilities and their families to lead 'normal' lives – to experience as far as possible the 'normal' pattern of being a child and being a parent – can be defined as the desire for inclusion. An inclusive society holds within itself a wide variety of people of different skills, talents and enthusiasms, of different backgrounds and of different abilities. Collectively, it makes provision for the needs – educational, social, recreational, medical – and beliefs of everyone, while recognising and valuing their differences. People with disabilities frequently find that society erects barriers to their participation and inclusion. These can be physical barriers or barriers of attitude. The refusal to recognise that a person with disabilities has as much as anyone else to contribute to society, and not purely on disability-related matters, is just as excluding as the flight of steps that prevents access to an office or a public building.

Inclusion can thus be defined as acceptance by society on one's own terms. For the children with disabilities, and their parents and wider families, who are the subject of this study, inclusion signifies recognising difference, accepting it and taking necessary action to ensure that difference does not create disadvantage.

Inclusion is not synonymous with integration. Integration is generally used to describe social and educational provision for children with disabilities alongside their non-disabled peers, i.e. in mainstream settings. In the educational context, inclusion means making the most appropriate provision for a child with disabilities. As the voices of the parents in this study make clear, for some children, and at some times, this may be as part of mainstream provision; at other times, a separate setting may better help a child with disabilities to flourish. The alternatives are not hard and fast for all time, even for a single individual.

Inclusion is a wider concept than integration, for it embraces the functioning of families and of societies. In the context of families with disabled children, especially young children, it covers such everyday but important issues as the roles of families and friends, and the assistance and support they provide; the impact of disability on non-disabled siblings; the practicality of getting out and about on family outings; the way in which intervention is organised; and the impact of attitudes held by the general public.

THE PARENTS' VIEW

Before finding out how far parents feel that their child with disabilities is included in all aspects of everyday family life, it was important to discover whether parents think that inclusion has any importance at all. If they view inclusion positively, why do they do so, and what does inclusion mean to individual families?

All the parents interviewed believe that inclusion in the wider community is essential for their children, irrespective of the nature or severity of their child's disability. Whether the children attend, or would in the future attend, mainstream or special schooling, parents feel that inclusion in at least some parts of their lives would enable them to sample as wide a range of experiences as anyone else, to enjoy life to the full and to prepare them for a future where people with disabilities are not segregated. Inclusion is also viewed as a basic human right:

> *I think everybody should be* [included] *– there shouldn't be any stipulations at all. Everyone should be together. I think she should try everything. Just because she doesn't walk or she doesn't talk, she* [shouldn't be denied] *the right to do anything she wants and just tone it down to work for her.*

> *I've always felt it very important that she is part of the world rather than part of the special needs world, because she eventually has to live in the world, not in cotton wool.*

> *They're still human beings. They should live a normal life as much as possible.*

Inclusion benefits everyone, and helps society to acknowledge the differences between people and to learn how to respond appropriately. Education and good example are the keys to successful inclusion and to accepting differences between people:

> *It gives other people a chance to see that everybody's different in the world. They're not all just – I hate the word 'normal', but 'everyday'. I think everybody should be aware there are people in the world with problems.*

> *The more people I can get involved with John, the better. I think everyone's got something to learn from it.*

Many parents feel that attitudes have changed since they were children, and that contemporary children's increased experiences of integrated schooling and inclusive play will help them to accept and understand disability in the future:

> *A lot of children now, say when they're three or four, have handicapped children around them every single day. As they get older, they learn to talk to them and properly respect them.*

> *I do think that society doesn't take account of people with*

disabilities unless they come into contact with them. They're not going to even think about them unless they actually see them, unless they're with them. I feel that should start in school. Children like Chloe aren't going to be able to go to a mainstream school, but I think schools should have, say, one afternoon a week where they let pupils mix and [they] get used to seeing children with disabilities.

It's very important for children with special needs to be included, for the basic reason that then people won't stop and stare when they see someone in a wheelchair. I think if they were in integrated schools from the beginning, then children are going to grow up with it and there's going to be no problem. As it is at the moment, you get people stopping and going, 'Mummy, why is that person in a wheelchair?' and it's very difficult.

The quality of inclusion is extremely important, so that both children with and without special needs get something positive out of the experience and neither side is exploited or restricted for the sake of the other. Good experiences of inclusion will lead to greater understanding, while a poor experience will be off-putting for everyone and deter people from planning inclusion, or participating, in the future:

[I want] integration, but somewhere that's really geared for special needs. My big thing is that she's really welcomed and wanted there, and not just there under sufferance.

All the integration that Jack has has got to be quality integration. It's important to me that through him integrating in a positive way with our help, then other children will find it easier. If it's not done in a positive and gentle way, then I think there will be a problem in the future. They will be included, but they will be put up with – and that's not what I want. I want more than that. It's okay including children with special needs, but if it alters the situation for children without special needs, then it creates a problem and it will never be successful. It's got to work so that children are not having to work too hard, otherwise it's not fair to the other children – they're not there for Jack's convenience.

Inclusion does not occur purely in formal, planned settings such as organised play or education. Inclusion means being part of a family, part of a social circle, part of the neighbourhood and of wider society. Inclusion is also an issue in the provision of support services and a suitable environment. It involves being visible, being accepted and participating as fully as possible:

I think it's down to parents and children themselves. You have to get your children out in their community. You do it like putting a stone in a pond and sending ripples out. You start with your parents and your family, close relatives, friends and neighbourhood, get your child out and get them known as an individual, get people to see through the slightly strange way they might walk or talk and to see the person within, and without being patronising.

Inclusion is a two-way process. Many parents have to make enormous efforts to enable inclusion of any kind to happen, but they also need society to welcome their efforts:

We do try as much as possible to be part of the community, but that depends on if the people in the community want to be part as well. You can only be part of the community if people really do want to be in it in the first place.

THE YOUNG PEOPLE'S VIEW

The young people with disabilities who took part in the research explored a number of issues around themselves, their self-image, and their feelings of inclusion and difference. On the whole, they felt that they experience quite different lives from their non-disabled contemporaries, although potentially they have many interests in common. Social networks are very important, both with friends and family with and without special needs.

It is difficult for the young people themselves, and for their families, to come to terms with their growing independence. Reasons for this include physical limitations and parental worries about safety in the wider community. Many young people with physical disabilities are keen to gain greater independence, to go out and about on their own like their non-disabled peers, and to have more choice and control over their activities. Those with learning disabilities are keen to continue with, and perhaps increase, activities they enjoy and mainly envisage doing this within the safety net of family support. Because they need to undertake activities that are appropriate both for their age and for their developmental level, there may be fewer ways in which they can be included on an equal footing with non-disabled young people of the same age. However, they enjoy being with family and with their friends with special needs, and this itself is a valuable form of inclusion.

It is noticeable that the young people in their later teens, who attended a residential unit, described significantly restricted opportunities, both in the unit and at home, in comparison with those enjoyed by their peers. At home, they are expected to join in with their parents' routines rather than with siblings or friends, in marked contrast with non-disabled young people of this age. Their aspirations are also limited, perhaps because they have little experience of ordinary adolescent life and are unaware of what their contemporaries aim to do in terms of further education and training, travel, work and leisure. The gap between disabled and non-disabled young people often widens in the later teenage years; for the young people with disabilities who live in a segregated setting, there are even fewer experiences and aims in common.

SAME AND DIFFERENT

Many of the things the young people liked, or disliked, about themselves and their lives are the same as non-disabled teenagers. This suggests that where disabled and non-disabled young people can be brought together, they will have some interests in common:

I like playing computer games. (Josh, aged 12)

I like going to book and comic shops and looking through all the books and comics. (Warren, aged 12)

I like playing the guitar and drums. I like playing football, I like practising outside. (Simon, aged 13)

I like going swimming and down the chutes. I like tenpin bowling. (Katy, aged 13)

I like listening to music and talking to my brother. (Rosie, aged 18)

I love books – experiencing romance! (Abigail, aged 12)

I wish I could have a telephone for my birthday because I'd like to talk to all my friends more. (Harriet, aged 13)

I like watching television and clapping when there's a goal. (Kim, aged 17)

I don't like getting out of bed in the morning. (Gail, aged 15)

I love art and maths and technology. (Georgina, aged 13)

I hate my skin. (Abigail, aged 12)

I hate my weight. (Andrew, aged 14)

Other things the disabled teenagers like have more in common with the activities enjoyed by younger non-disabled children:

I like playing in the garden on the swing. I like teddybears. (Natasha, aged 13)

I like making buses out of Lego. (Warren, aged 12)

I like playing in my bedroom with wind-up toys. (Katy, aged 13)

A number expressed dislikes that centre on their disability and the feelings of difference that it creates:

I dislike my leg – it gives up. (Veronica, aged 14)

My shoes are big and I don't like my legs. I don't like my boots. (Daniel, aged 13)

I'm different because I'm bent over. (Toni, aged 14)

Other people can go out by themselves and I have to stay indoors. I'd like to go with them. It is different [when you're disabled] *because my brother has gone off to play and I am left in. I'd like to be able to go out with him. I am different because other people do more than me ... I feel a bit jealous because everyone walks.* (Charlie, aged 19)

I didn't like PHAB [Physically Handicapped and Able Bodied club] *on a Thursday because of the attitude, and someone called me a spastic.* (Rosie, aged 18)

People outside [my residential placement] *make me feel different because they can walk and we can't.* (Clare, aged 18)

Even within a group of disabled young people, it is possible to feel separate:

I think I'm different because I have a disability which is different to everyone else. (Andrew, aged 14)

However, being different is not always perceived as a disadvantage:

I think it is different for young people with disabilities and I like being different. (Lucy, aged 18)

The way I live is different, but I like it. (Martin, aged 13)

And not all feelings of difference stem from disability:

I like being on my own. This makes me different. (Veronica, aged 14)

I'm different because I laugh a lot. (Toni, aged 14)

Not everyone feels different all the time:

I do the same sort of things as other children. I don't feel I do anything different. (Elizabeth, aged 13)

My house is just like anybody's house – we argue, we fight, we cry, we laugh. (Andrew, aged 14)

I feel the same as other young people because I argue with my brother. (Veronica, aged 14)

EXPANDING HORIZONS

Inclusion can mean mixing with both disabled and non-disabled peers, and joining in with what they do. It also means having the opportunity to participate in similar activities and to enjoy similar experiences separately from non-disabled peers.

The young people with disabilities described more limited experiences than those available to non-disabled teenagers. Almost all the special events they attend are family based, which parallels the social experiences of younger children (see Chapter 4). However, they are included as part of their extended family, in contrast with some younger disabled children (see Chapter 5).

These were the responses when participants were asked to name a favourite special event:

I went to a big New Year's Eve party with the family.
(Elizabeth, aged 13)

I've visited a new baby in my family. (Gordon, aged 14)

My aunt's wedding when I was six. (Daniel, aged 13)

My grandad's 75th birthday party. (Veronica, aged 14)

I went to my cousin's engagement party and a cousin's wedding. I went to my cousin's first birthday party and a party for my mother passing her driving test. (Hannah, aged 12)

Only a few other, non family-based, special events were mentioned:

November the fifth at Lewes fireworks. (Robert, aged 13)

My dad bought me a guitar. I went with him to the music shop. I enjoyed being in the shop. I chose it myself. (Simon, aged 13)

The young people's own birthday parties are a highlight. However, as with younger disabled children (see Chapter 4), birthday parties, in particular for young people with learning disabilities, consist of relatives rather than the teenager's own friends:

I like cakes with candles, crisps, chocolate. I feel all right on my birthday. (Natasha, aged 13)

Mummy, daddy, my brothers and sisters come to my party. (Dominic, aged 12)

I like the special dinner that my mummy cooks for me on my birthday. I like the balloons on the kitchen ceiling, getting dressed in my best clothes for my special birthday dinner. I like spending my birthday with mummy, daddy and nanny. (Gail, aged 15)

Some of the young people wanted more independence than they are currently allowed. They felt that non-disabled teenagers go out more than they do and so have access to a wider range of experiences.

Being disabled is different because they do more than I do. It makes me feel frustrated. (Clare, aged 18)

The things other people do, I want to do as well – like walking down to the shops. It makes me feel cross. (Lucy, aged 18)

I want to go out more but my parents won't let me. They think it's safe for me to stay in. This is because I have a disability, but I know when I get tired now. (Veronica, aged 14)

I think some parents are too overprotective. (Elizabeth, aged 13)

Young people with disabilities don't go out so much. (Daniel, aged 13)

Daniel's friend commented:

I agree with Daniel. Some people's parents are worried about them if they go out. If they have fits, they are worried a car would go over them if the driver didn't know they were having a fit. (Georgina, aged 13)

[About not going out so much] *Some people say it's because of my age, but I think it's because of my disability.* (Georgina, aged 13)

Sometimes, seemingly quite small things stop young people with disabilities being independent and like other teenagers:

I can't do my hi-fi myself, which I'd like to do. I like my stereo up full-blast in the morning. (Clare, aged 18)

The young people want to use increased independence to expand their horizons in parallel with other people of their age:

I want to go into town on my own. (Toni, aged 14)

I'd like to go to the cinema on my own. (Robert, aged 13)

I'd like to go to a nightclub. (Clare, aged 18)

I'd like to go into town whenever I want, and have more responsibilities. (Veronica, aged 14)

A fairly restricted range of after-school and weekend activities was mentioned:

We go to the shops and I go to [the residential unit's weekend house]. *It's just down the road. It's where you go to get away from school if you don't go home to your mum and dad. We do more at school than when we go there.* (Clare, aged 18)

I normally go home [from the residential placement] *at weekends. I sit at home watching t.v. – it's a bit boring. Sometimes I want to stay at school.* (Charlie, aged 19)

When I go home we go shopping and I watch videos. I go out to church. When we are at school [at weekends] *we choose where we want to go. I like shopping and I like to go to parks.*
(Rosie, aged 18)

I go to the shops and I go to church. I think my weekends are different [being disabled]. *I'd like to go out on my own.*
(Lucy, aged 18)

I like the pie shop, I like the smell of the shop. I like my daddy taking me in my wheelchair. (Harriet, aged 13)

Social networks are important in leisure time:

I see some of my friends – sometimes I do, sometimes I don't.
(Josh, aged 12)

I like going to PHAB [Physically Handicapped and Able Bodied club] *because it's one of the places I meet my boyfriend.*
(Lucy, aged 18)

I like PHAB because it's with able-bodied people. They don't come to school here. That's why I like going. They're all about my age. I go once a week. (Rosie, aged 18)

I go to Venture Scouts at school. I like it because there are more adult people, there are things to do and it's interesting. I go out, go on camp holidays for a week, play games. We do different things every week and it stays interesting. (Clare, aged 18)

School also provides valuable social networks:

I like everything about the journey to school. I don't feel different about it because I go with lots of people. I leave home and cross the road and into the woods, mess about, and then come back the same way. There are seven of us. (Martin, aged 13)

I like seeing all my friends on the journey [in the minibus to school]. *I like hearing the other children talking.* (Gail, aged 15)

Some young people want to do more of activities they have already sampled. Others want to try something completely new:

I wish I could go swimming more often. (Katy, aged 13)

I'd like to go to a youth club that's near home. (Elizabeth, aged 13)

I'd like to go back to the Brecon Beacons and go down a coal mine, and abseiling with the mountain rescue team.
(Abigail, aged 12)

I'd like to go ice-skating and I'd like to do something outrageous, like bungee-jumping. (Hannah, aged 12)

I'd like to go fishing every day, bungee-jumping and sky-diving.
(Martin, aged 13)

I wish I could go to the pub, drink and smoke, like a grown up.
(Simon, aged 13)

When asked what they might like to do in the future, the older ones said:

I'd like to go to college, I don't know what I'd do there.
(Rosie, aged 18)

I'd like to go to college. (Lucy, aged 18)

I'd like to have joined the Territorial Army, but they wouldn't let me because I use a wheelchair. (Charlie, aged 19)

Two answers show that the lives of young people with disabilities are likely to be very different from those of able-bodied young people:

I'd like to live somewhere I could live independently. Perhaps a small bungalow, not a big building. (Charlie, aged 19)

I'd like to go to R. H., a residential home I'm hoping to go to.
(Clare, aged 18)

SUMMARY

All the parents felt that inclusion in the family, neighbourhood and wider society was essential for children with disabilities to enable them to participate as fully as possible in ordinary, everyday life, develop skills and interests, and be accepted in their own right. Parents believe that well-planned, quality inclusion, including integrated schooling and inclusive play, can benefit the whole of society by imparting greater awareness and acceptance of difference.

The young people with disabilities were able to give a brief taste of what their lives are like. Almost more important, however, was what was left out. Without choices and a variety of experiences, it is not possible to say what one would really prefer or hope to do; for most young disabled people, the lack of choice and variety was demonstrated by the more limited horizons to which they could aspire.

CHAPTER *3*

The struggle for a normal family life

Families, and particularly parents, are the key to children's wider horizons. This is true of all young children, disabled or otherwise: parental expectations and resources determine how much or how little they do both inside and outside the home. However, a child with learning difficulties or with severe mobility problems will rely on his or her parents for far longer, if not indefinitely. Families play a vital role in encouraging and nurturing their disabled child to develop independence, and enabling this process to happen successfully.

The family's overall health – physical, mental and emotional – is a crucial factor. It underpins the wellbeing of the disabled child and the opportunities available to him or her. While formal support systems exist in both the statutory and voluntary sectors to help families with a disabled child, families have their own personal networks as well – relatives, friends, neighbours and colleagues – who may provide support in many different ways. This chapter looks at how far these networks provide the required support, to the family as a whole, before going on to discuss how much children with disabilities are able to be included in ordinary, everyday family life.

GETTING A BREAK

In all families, parents get a break from their children from time to time – and children from their parents. Children have to learn to live without constant contact with their parents and to have new, and slightly different, experiences from when they are with their parents. This is the start of the long process that leads to eventual independence. Parents, too, need 'time off' – even if it is only to do other non-parenting work around the house.

For families with a disabled child, a break is even more important: some form of respite care is essential if they are to have an ordinary family life. Parents need respite care – whether organised informally through family and friends, or formally through voluntary or statutory agencies – for a variety of reasons:

- to do ordinary domestic tasks, which are difficult or impossible to carry out while caring for a child with special needs;

- to spend time with their other children and meet their needs;

- to meet their own needs (work, health care, rest, relaxation) and to maintain other personal relationships.

The need is especially acute among parents of preschool-age children, who are at home all the time. Once children start attending school, the situation eases slightly.

For all the parents in the survey, finding good, reliable care for a disabled child is much more complicated than it is for their other non-disabled children. In every family, respite care is a major concern, both in the present and looking towards the future:

People who come into the home are so important because they give you a break and you can get away from the responsibility of looking after your child all the time, and then come back with renewed vigour. Because it's for ever, looking after a handicapped person is for ever. It's not like having a normal child who will go off at eighteen ... a handicapped person, they're there till you die, and then you are worrying about what's going to happen after you die. So you never lose that, it's there all the time.

The need for a break is much greater because the tasks involved in caring for a disabled child are more onerous than ordinary child care:

That's the thing I've noticed more now, having another child, that there is no switch-off time. With Catherine you just don't switch off at all, you've always got to be 'on the ball'. It's very tiring because I can't let her get on by herself. Mentally, it's very tiring, apart from physically tiring. I can never really relax, not as I can with [her younger sister]. You need to recharge your batteries, you know, you should be able to actually relax.

INFORMAL NETWORKS

Many parents said that it is difficult to find someone they feel confident they can trust with the care of their child. Initially, parents – of any child, disabled or not – tend to look to their extended family for help. Many grandparents cannot wait to look after their grandchildren and so parents do not feel that they are asking for a favour.

However, this kind of support for a child with special needs is not always forthcoming. Families who can rely on help from close relations regard this as a real bonus, but they are not in the majority:

> If I hadn't had my parents, I don't think I would have survived Clare's early years. They love her to bits and can't wait to have her.

> His grandmother, she's great, she's had him since he was six weeks old, one night a week, and I don't have to think about him at all then.

> My brother moved down from the Midlands to help me out, which is brilliant. He's really helping Harry all he can, he's really positive and a real strength.

Many parents find that the disability makes grandparents or other relatives reluctant to look after their child. Sometimes relatives are concerned about coping with a child's medical problems or his or her unfamiliar needs. However, on occasions, parents feel that the reluctance stems from a lack of understanding of the child and what is required for his or her care:

> Everybody wants to see Chloe, all the family. On the practical side, though, the offers aren't there to look after her. I think they're frightened, frightened of doing the wrong thing. They think she's fragile because she's got a lot of problems.

> It's normally grandparents who baby-sit when we go out. About a year ago, Nicholas had to wear night-splints on his legs. It was difficult to find baby-sitters then because he had to be splinted up. My dad wouldn't put the night-splints on him – he wouldn't put them on his grandson. He probably thinks it's a bit unfair. [But] if he didn't wear his night-splints, in the morning he wouldn't be able to walk because his legs would have got stuck in one position.

Friends sometimes provide support, although awareness of the child's needs is crucial. But all too often friends are reluctant to step in and parents are unwilling to ask:

We've got friends who have known Tim since he was born, who see how we handle him, and they're quite confident that they can cope with him as well.

I have left her with close friends and they will cope, but nobody likes it and I daren't ask, really. It's not that they don't like doing it, it's just that they're so worried because she has got really funny movements and her feeding is terrible, especially for somebody who doesn't know her.

Parents feel that there are relatively few people they can trust to cope with their child's special needs. Lack of awareness or practical expertise in people they might ordinarily ask to baby-sit limits their choices. They have to feel confident that their child is in good hands, otherwise they would not leave the child with anyone. If they are worrying, they are unable to relax and getting away is not worth the effort or the risk:

They've really got to know John and know his epilepsy if it happens, and know about his sleeping patterns and the way to hold him. So really, it's both our mums and the lady from the hospital. It's got to be someone you really trust.

Anyone that's offered to baby-sit, if they've got children without any problems they haven't got a clue what to do with him. Because if he wakes up he can't turn over by himself, he can't do anything for himself and they would expect him to be able to do a certain amount. They wouldn't think that he'd choke if he was on his back, or he wouldn't just be able to get a drink and go back to sleep.

Daytime or overnight care by family or friends is often impossible to organise:

The problem would be leaving him somewhere during the day or if we wanted to get away. We know we could leave his sisters, but the problem would be Tim. We've never been able to leave him for a day, or a day and an evening, or maybe a weekend, with anybody.

There is no one that could have her for a night.

As a result, many parents have never had more than a couple of hours off at a time since their child was born. Nor, given the likelihood of continuing dependence, can they foresee that this will change. The informal, often reciprocal, child care that occurs among parents of young children without special needs does not develop if a child has a disability:

No one ever rings up and says, 'Can Tim come round?' or, 'Can we take Tim off your hands for a day?', whereas with the girls it does happen.

People have often said they'd have William [brother without special needs]. I've always said, 'Oh, yes, that's kind of you,' but it will always be – what can I do with Georgia? And they like to be together anyway, it's not fair to separate them.

FORMAL RESPITE CARE

The families interviewed received formal respite care from a variety of sources, including:

- Family Link, family-based respite care organised by social services;

- Crossroads Carers' Scheme, a voluntary organisation offering short-term carers in the home to anyone caring for a child or adult with disabilities;

- a baby-sitting service run from the local children's hospital, providing trained personnel, usually nurses, for children with specific medical problems.

Families feel that access to this kind of care is essential:

You need somewhere. I think some people manage without, I never know how they do. I think they must have very supportive families. It's not that ours haven't wanted to help, but they haven't been able to.

We haven't had any respite care, not since Joanne [now aged 4]

*was born. I think something like that should be available to all
parents with children with special needs. It's a definite need.*

A number of parents expressed confidence in such carers, either
because of their experience with special needs or because they are
willing to acquire it:

*I am very particular about baby-sitters. We actually use an
organisation called Crossroads. We have a lovely lady who
comes twice a month so we actually get to go out. She is really
good and James really likes her. I feel quite happy to leave him
with her.*

[The Family Link parent] *is really good with John. She's had him
when his epilepsy is bad so she knows what to look for. She
always used to say, 'If he has a fit I'm frightened I'm going to
miss it.' But I said, 'You won't. If it happens you won't.' But she
was convinced until it did* [happen] *and she said she'd never have
mistaken that.*

Parents who have used holiday playschemes, nurseries and child-
minders often speak very positively about them:

Simon went to an integrated playscheme two days a week [in the
school holiday]. *It was a real success. It just saved my life, the
days he went there.*

*She goes to a childminder and she's brilliant. Her sister adopts
children with special needs so she can borrow a lot of equipment
from her sister.*

Having regular, reliable respite care is vital in helping parents to win
some free time and develop their own life:

*I now have somebody coming in on Friday mornings for four hours
from Crossroads and she looks after the children while I go out,
which is very useful. It gives me time to go to the doctor's, have
my hair done, dentist appointments, things like that. And
occasionally I'll go off and have a swim.*

*The link family, that's every other week for a day, which is good.
In a day you can do so much.*

Some families manage to use respite care to enable everyone else to go away together on holiday:

> [Before] *Sarah has come on holiday with us, but this year we didn't take her with us because* [the residential respite care centre] *covered it. They do a week at a time. I must say we did realise that, although we miss Sarah, she does stop us doing things.*

Parents feel that good respite care can offer their child many positive experiences. If it does not, they would feel guilty and would not be happy to use it:

> *Because she's had some respite care in the last two years, that meant that she has been going off with groups* [of people] *like her and they've done lots of things, they're very good at taking them out.*

> *I would have to feel that Simon was happy, then I wouldn't feel guilty because of going* [out].

However, there are drawbacks. While parents are grateful for the respite care they receive, they identified problems, such as long waits for care to be organised and reductions or breaks in service. They also suggested improvements, for example, greater flexibility in making provision for the whole family:

> [The care] *is three hours, which is okay, but you can't wander too far because you're not there for long before you're coming back.*

> *We haven't ever been out* [as a couple], *we haven't ever been out since we had Joanne, we don't go out. A lady told me about this scheme, but they wouldn't look after your other siblings, so we can't* [use that].

Parents of very disabled children do not appear to take up family-based respite care. Reasons include the feeling that their child's needs are too great for volunteers to meet on a regular basis, and fears for the child's safety:

> *We have never felt confident in something like a link family because Joanne is so demanding, it can be so stressful. I can't*

imagine what it would be like with a normal family who are, I'm sure, very careful, I can't imagine them bearing it. It takes a saint to look after Joanne when she's bad.

I've always been wary of the Family Link scheme because Christina hasn't got any verbal language. I always worried about her going into somebody's house because although the family – the actual link person – would be vetted by social services, you never know who else is going to be invited into that person's house while your child is there.

Stresses and strains grow when families have a long wait for help, experience interrupted care, or feel unable to make use of existing services. Several families described situations that would seem intolerable to outsiders:

Look at our situation – we've been at home for four years, that is a long time, not being able to do anything, go anywhere, get up and go any time we want to. You just learn to live like that, you learn to do it, humans adapt to everything. In the beginning it was hell, but right now we're used to it.

Several parents commented on the complexity of getting any kind of care and wished that for once it could be straightforward. Some families have quite simple needs that are not being met:

With your ordinary children, it's so easy, playgroup at two and a half, you just go. I think there should be something like that for children with Joanne's needs, just for a couple of hours, just go and pay a fee like we do with the other children. We could have a break for a couple of hours. I think that would be wonderful.

If I could have someone for two hours a week, to take him to gym club, to take him to his swimming lessons – that's what I'd dearly love.

Parents cannot always look forward to a time when their child will no longer need other carers – appropriate care may be required indefinitely. This creates worries about the impact of spending cuts:

We have a girl who comes in every week to look after Lottie and those hours have been cut ... I think they place a huge reliance on parents and husbands and wives to look after people, and that's what makes me so cross about [cutting funding for] *things like Crossroads, which is such a cheap alternative and does so much for families. I think community care has got to be improved or families are not going to be able to cope. They are just going to fall apart, and then what happens? The child has to go into care, which costs a fortune. What is upsetting from my point of view is that so many children in Lottie's school are in care.*

PLANNING FOR THE WHOLE FAMILY

Parents were asked how the specialist services provided for their child with a disability fitted in with the needs of the rest of the family. Their answers overwhelmingly dealt with the practical difficulties that arose, particularly with children of preschool age.

Many families feel that provision for their disabled child fails to take into account that a young child is likely to be part of a young family. Some 80 per cent of disabled children in the study had siblings, usually close in age. However, the child with special needs is often treated in isolation, just like any adult patient, regardless of his or her needs resulting both from being a child and being part of a young family. This created too many additional complications and stresses for families. Parents recognise that many services are fully stretched in terms of both time and money, and that this reduces flexibility. Nevertheless, proper planning and co-ordination of services, taking into account that young children often come as part of a family package, would lead to better use of the existing limited resources.

LOCATION AND TIMING

While parents often make great efforts to enable their child to benefit from specialist input, the arrangements often create additional strain for themselves and their families. Appointment times do not necessarily reflect the child's or the family's needs: a parent with other school-age children might be offered a regular 8.30 a.m. session, or after-school sessions, which exclude school-age siblings. Sometimes, parents cannot see any way around the problem, apart from withdrawing from the help that their child needs, which they are naturally reluctant to do.

Many parents feel guilty about not taking up sessions, or requesting more convenient schedules, and are often afraid that their child might have to wait longer if they do not accept what is first offered. They also feel that they might be branded as 'awkward parents' and that consequently their child may suffer. There is no evidence of this happening, but parents nevertheless feel under additional pressure:

> The appointments are difficult. I find it difficult to understand why they don't ask you when it's most convenient and try and fit in with when they will get the most out of the child, which they don't do. That's a pain because you've wasted your time and you've wasted their time.

> Her treatment is led from [a town] eighty miles away. I would have to spend one day a week up there because of the exercise and routine there. The journey would take four hours, but it was just too much for a young baby [Stephanie's sister] as well as being able to deal with Stephanie who is in even more pain having been in the car. I was so distressed and worn out by the time I came back.

TRANSPORT AND ACCESS

Parents without their own transport commented on the long waits for hospital transport, which ignores the needs of young children, to and from appointments. If a parent gets a child awake, fed, washed, dressed and in a clean nappy, and then has to wait for transport to arrive, they may begin to ask if it is all worth it. Similarly, a long wait after the appointment before going home can lead to problems if the child is hungry or tired, and to worries about other children who have to be fetched from school or child care. The inflexibility of the system can mean that some families cannot take up services:

> You do get hospital transport to go up to the hospital, but it would just be the time – you have to wait for someone to come and pick you up and take you. I'd rather walk, I'd rather walk up there than wait for a car.

We didn't have a car. The hospital transport wouldn't take her baby sister as well, so I would have to take both children, walk to a friend's house, drop her sister off, walk back with Stephanie, wait for up to an hour for hospital transport to come, go to the physio session, and then we'd have to go and collect her sister. It was a very unhelpful arrangement and I just said, 'No, thank you – we'll just carry on at home.' The hospital system only looked at Stephanie, they didn't have the flexibility to include us as a family.

Physical access to buildings also creates problems both for children in wheelchairs and for those in ordinary pushchairs:

If I go to the doctor's, then I can park quite close and I carry him across the road ... When I'm actually in the doctor's surgery, I'll just put him on the floor. It's not always very pleasant for him but you just have to do that, don't you, sometimes? The palaver of getting a wheelchair out and strapping him in it – it's just easier to carry him in and plonk him on the floor.

At the doctor's, they've got double doors. You can't actually get the buggy through so you have to open both doors and shove him through. You get the odd person who'll hold the door open, but on the whole people try their damnedest not even to register that you're there and just blank it out.

Managing children

Waiting to be seen at an appointment can also be difficult. It is hard to manage a child with special needs, and harder still to manage more than one child, in a waiting room or corridor, especially if there is a long time to wait. The difficulties are greater with services designed for the general population, such as hospital ear, nose and throat departments or GP surgeries, than in those aimed specifically at children. Poor facilities cause stress, and make parents feel that the assessments are useless because they and their disabled child cannot make the most of them:

The waiting room for the ear, nose and throat department has an open door and Katy is constantly running out of there and I'm constantly running after her, and we have to wait such a long time from the actual appointment time to seeing anybody. Katy does get very restless and I'm chasing after her.

One parent commented that a service aimed at children with disabilities had less child-friendly arrangements than the nearby children's outpatients' area and also appeared to be segregating these children unnecessarily:

In his first year, to get his six-month check-up, we used to go to outpatients. There was a lovely charity-run place where you could get a cup of tea, there was a lovely big waiting area with lots of toys for the children. Your name was called and you could wheel the pushchair down the ramp and into the room. Now, you go to the specialist centre which is for the disabled and if you're seen for a six-month check-up, you have to go upstairs. There's nowhere to put the pushchairs, and you have to leave them downstairs and carry him up. I can't understand why you're separated like that. We talk about exclusion and inclusion. There is no earthly reason why we shouldn't have a six-monthly check-up in the normal outpatients' department, unless they want to label him disabled.

Yet some parents find solutions to at least some of these difficulties. Establishing good relations with staff helps – and sometimes it is just luck that makes all the difference:

It's difficult if I'm going [to the doctor's] *for me because I have to leave her somewhere. I have to lie her on the floor in there. They usually get pillows out. Most of the secretaries know Chloe now so they usually hold her. Someone will help out while you're there.*

Our doctor had a child of his own with special needs so he totally sympathises with us, which is a real bonus.

Forward planning is also essential, but this means finding someone to help. As we have already seen, this can turn into an added burden, given people's reluctance to offer to look after a disabled child:

I've arranged that both their [two children with learning disabilities] *appointments are at the same time so that makes it easier, but when they have to have hearing tests, then I have to arrange for somebody else to look after one of them.*

ON THE MERRY-GO-ROUND

Parents say that, as soon as you discover that your child has a disability, you are sucked into a whirlwind of activity centred on assessment and intensive therapeutic input. While parents are grateful for all the help they can get, the demands of the schedule can impose great strains on the family:

We fit round him, we really do. We fit totally round John. We gave up our jobs to fit round John. Everything is just John at the moment, his treatments, everything geared up to John, the whole day.

When Lottie was first diagnosed, I felt I had to do everything for her – she would be going to the sensory group, to physio once a week, and I'd have the Portage worker, the peripatetic teacher and the speech therapist coming here, and I used to go swimming with her every week. It was like this burden I had, I felt so guilty about that I just had to do everything. I was on a frantic merry-go-round and I just collapsed in a heap one day and I couldn't manage it all. I also felt I was losing sight of Lottie, I was doing all those things and yet I was losing sight of her as a person. That's when I started easing back a bit.

Much more is asked of children with disabilities than of non-disabled children. Although they may find learning and physical activities difficult, tiring and even painful, disabled children are expected to do more than their non-disabled peers. They have to accommodate in their lives physical therapies, learning programmes, developmental assessments and more medical check-ups and tests, as well as find time for ordinary things such as play, rest and relaxation. This is particularly true for very young children; for older children, some of these things can be absorbed into the school timetable.

Children with disabilities are also asked to interact with a larger number of adults – and if possible to interact meaningfully to assist assessment or therapy. They are expected to cope with a variety of different settings from an early age, even though we know that children with a learning disability find it hard to pick up information and generalise skills in unfamiliar surroundings. Disabled children may have to put up with unpleasant medical procedures and operations, and to separate from their parents when still very young to attend specialist preschool provision. Later, they may have to cope with long journeys on school transport and long days away from home if they have to travel out of the neighbourhood to special educational provision.

This frantic merry-go-round can all too easily exclude children from experiencing ordinary life. It can also prevent parents feeling like 'normal parents' and provoke a great deal of guilt – a word that was used during many interviews. Parents feel under enormous pressure to provide their children with the opportunities, in the form of specialised activities and input, that will help them to fulfil their potential. Even though many of them describe a regime into which it would be hard to fit anything more, parents feel guilty that they do not do enough and guilty if they or their child take time off:

> *Every night I go to bed and think I haven't done this or that today. There's always that guilt, I mean terrible guilt.*

> *I've got to give him this chance and try and do as much as we can and get it all in. Because when he's older and asks me, 'Why can't I walk?' or, 'Why can't I do this?', then I've got to be able to say to him, 'We tried everything we could and we gave it a good bash.' At least I won't be able to say, 'Well, you didn't want to do it at the time, so I thought: we'll sit at home, all snugly.' You know there's no point in that.*

> *If I'm tidying up in the morning and he's lying with the t.v. or the video on; and I'm rushing about and thinking, 'Oh, he's been there for an hour, he's not really doing anything', you get such a guilt feeling, you know, you must get up and do something about it. But they do need their own time to just kick around and just be 'me', if you like, rather than 24 hours a day constant stimulation.*

A SENSE OF PERSPECTIVE

Some parents feel that, with the benefit of experience, they manage to achieve a perspective on the relative value of specialised input and spending ordinary time with their child:

I do think it's a stage everyone goes through when their child's diagnosed. You're just shell-shocked and you rush around doing all these things. I used to think if I do all these things and if I make her do it, she'll do it. And then I suddenly realised that no amount of willpower on my part was going to make her do it.

Nevertheless, especially when their disabled child is also their first child, parents can be plunged into a world of 'special needs' without experiencing ordinary parenthood or achieving an ordinary childhood for their child:

Now, having Jane and seeing what she's doing, I feel Catherine has definitely missed out because she's not able to do the [same] things, she hasn't really enjoyed a proper childhood ... Playing becomes a chore because you're playing very structured games and trying to teach her things. I think in the end it becomes more of a chore than a game. Having Jane now has brought it back to being games again.

Some parents feel that their experience of raising other children enables them to put things into perspective:

I'm lucky, I have a [grown up] child so I've been through it all, but a parent who it's their first child, I wonder how they cope. They don't know that they have the option to say, 'No, we won't do this today because this child has had too much.'

Other parents feel that it would be useful to have it emphasised that their child with disabilities is a child first, with the needs of any young child, but with additional needs arising from the disability:

We've never been in a meeting or a discussion group where someone's said, 'Your child is a normal child, treat it like you would any other child, do things with it, enjoy that child and make sure that child enjoys as broad a scope of activities as possible.'

'IF YOU DON'T DO IT, NO ONE ELSE WILL'

Parents have to devote an enormous amount of time to getting the outside support they feel their child needs: another way in which their lives differ from those of other parents. The word 'fight' occurs frequently:

There's always a lot of paperwork to be sorting out, chasing people all the time. That's the worst side of it. Usually that's done in the evening when John's gone to bed and we're both so tired that we don't want to do it. There's just not enough hours in the day. And it has to be done, letters off to people, sorting out John's needs, because if you don't do it, no one else will.

We've got to finance wheelchairs, walkers and stuff, and people think it comes from the government and it doesn't. You have to find the money yourself. We've been lucky in getting the money [for his special walking frame] *but not everyone is. We probably won't be so lucky with his wheelchair.*

Parents do not feel that the necessary information is always easy to obtain. Despite the increased number of information services and directories, there is still a long way to go to improve the situation:

There's a lot of pressure, you feel on your own a lot of the time when you're fighting for things. Some things you don't get a lot of help with, and sometimes you don't know where to go next. You just stumble around until you find the answer.

There is a lot of help available, but it takes a very long time to get it. There's too many procedures, there's too many forms to fill, there's too much hassle.

Several parents describe how their personalities changed as they learnt to deal with new situations:

It's a shame everything's a fight. It's just such a battle, as if we haven't got enough to do, enough to worry about. There's always added things to do, to have to fight for – literally to have to fight for – and you've got to speak up. If you're quiet and shy you've had it, so you find yourselves being aggressive. I'm a lot more aggressive now than I was, simply because I'm so used to doing it to people when I need things.

I was brought up to be very polite, to always act appropriately, say the right thing. When you have an autistic child, you don't always [do that]. *I've learnt to just brazen it out.*

BROTHERS AND SISTERS

Eighty per cent of the children in the study had one or more siblings – some as many as five. The presence of other children in the family presents some of the best opportunities for including a disabled child in ordinary, everyday family life. Yet siblings also give rise to some of the most difficult situations with which parents have to contend.

Having a brother or sister with special needs can affect children in many different ways. Parents are acutely aware of this and make a great deal of effort to try to understand the problems their non-disabled children face and, whenever possible, to minimise the disadvantages.

The time and energy parents have to spend on meeting the needs of their disabled child, both at home and outside, has an impact on siblings. Where and when they go on family outings can be restricted, as can the outside activities to which their parents take them. Plans can be disrupted because the disabled child's needs have to take priority. Above all, parents feel that their other children suffer because so much attention is focused on the disabled child.

Society's attitudes to disability also affect siblings. Siblings can have problems with bringing friends home and with how these friends respond, and with wanting, or not wanting, to include the disabled child in their activities with friends. Siblings are also concerned about the longer-term implications of the disability, in particular its impact on their own lives and on their decisions about having children.

OPENING UP THE WORLD

In families where the disabled child is the oldest, the arrival of later siblings without disabilities creates links with the ordinary world that parents have either been unable to make before, or have not known how to:

> *It's good for us* [having another child, Jane] *because it means that we're not just going everywhere that is different and special and for children with special needs. We are actually integrating into the community having Jane because she's playing with children and so we're talking more to their parents, and then we're not quite so much the odd ones out. We were very much the people with the handicapped child, but now, well, we're Jane's parents. It makes you come back to normality.*

He doesn't demand to go, say, to the park, so it doesn't bother me if I don't go. Whereas hopefully Anna [younger sister] will be saying, 'Ooh, swings, swings!' and it'll make me have to take them to the park.

Parents regard the presence of another child or children in the immediate family as immensely beneficial to the disabled child. It is the first real step towards inclusion. Siblings can provide fun and enjoyment, friendship and stimulation for the child with disabilities:

She's actually watching what [her brother] *does now. Before, she used to just sit there, but now she's watching him running around.*

Jane's been brilliant for her, it's the best thing we could ever have done. She crawls all over the floor and they kiss and cuddle and scratch each other, and all that sort of thing, but it's marvellous.

Brothers and sisters bring their friends into the house and so extend the disabled child's circle in a way that the child may not be able to achieve her-/himself:

Lottie loves having [her brother's] *friends around. She loves other children and she's just happy to watch and laugh and be involved in what they're up to.*

At mothers-and-toddlers, the other children are talking to Jane and then they automatically come and talk to Catherine as well.

Some parents commented that their other children, not just their disabled child, have benefited:

They adore Sarah. It brings out the good in them as well, that you don't always see between other siblings. It gives you faith in humanity, how they are much nicer to each other when they realise there is a problem. And it's taught them a lot about handicap.

Other children in the family supply parents – and children – with a model of the kind of activities they can aspire to, and can even pave the way where parents did not expect the disabled child to follow. However, at times the contrasts can be very painful:

[Her brother] has just joined Beavers so she's very keen on

joining something. As soon as she's five she can join something like Girls' Brigade and things like that would be quite nice for her. And now she's been to a small dance class and coped quite well with it, and she's very keen to go again. With our son, we tried to get him involved in after-school interests, and it starts off with just physical things like Tumble-Tots and gym. We wanted to do the same sort of process with her and this is really the first one.

[His older brothers] were in Cubs and I wanted Joseph to be a Cub more than anything. Even though I knew he wouldn't be able to start at eight, I thought he'd be able to start at nine and they'd make allowances for him. But his behaviour at the moment is so awful that I wouldn't [take him].

Sometimes the contrast in available opportunities stems from the attitudes of other people rather than from any obstacles caused by the disability:

There was one incident which made me a little sad. Some friends rang up and said, 'We'd like you to come over.' They had a little boy about six weeks younger than Georgia and obviously he likes to run around with William [older brother]. I said, 'William's actually over at a friend's,' and he said, 'Oh, well, I hope you won't take offence but as it's just Georgia, she won't be too much company for Richard.' She's a bright little girl, the only difference is that she can't run around as quickly.

It was her birthday. My brother didn't get her a card or anything. Didn't even 'phone to say happy birthday to her. Didn't even come to the door and say, 'Happy birthday, Carly'. There was nothing. Neil's [Carly's brother] always had a card, they've even come to his birthday party.

CONFLICTS OF INTEREST

Parents often find that the needs of a disabled child and non-disabled siblings compete and conflict, thus creating tension. Parents are clear that having a disabled brother or sister restricts the lives of their other children. Difficult behaviour, the need for sensitive management of the disabled child's routine and personal care, and a busy schedule of specialised input for the disabled child are all reasons why other children lose out:

> If Joanne isn't well we can't go out, we have to stay in. If we take her to the park when she has quite bad epilepsy and she's fitting, that can be very awkward and we have to bring her home, so it definitely does affect our other children. People get frightened and they do react to it, and you feel awkward, and of course it ruins the whole enjoyment with our other children.

> It was difficult for William. It's been much easier since she's gone to [special school] because so much of the training and therapy [takes place there]. Before, a lot of it took place here or there was a rush after William was picked up from school. So he was either being carted around in Georgia's wake and had to go somewhere where all the interest was on Georgia, or people would come here and again assess her and encourage her. And he'd be really a bit of a marginal, peripheral figure and sometimes he'd try for a bit more attention, and that was jolly difficult because he was only three or four years old.

Parents struggle to meet the needs of all their children and are aware that their non-disabled children may be disadvantaged. Managing the tensions – an organisational and emotional balancing act – requires much parental effort. Parents are acutely sensitive to the demands that one child's disability makes on their other children. This can affect even the most apparently trivial things and gives parents more to cope with at every level of existence:

> It's not that he inhibits being able to do things, it's just that when you're doing things, you're having to concentrate on him. In the holiday we went fishing, which wasn't easy, but we did it. But I had to hold Tim the whole time, and the rod, and I couldn't help his sisters. They actually get quite annoyed with him. He gets all the attention. They're really good with him and they love him, but they're young as well. Ideally, they should have a third of my attention each, but they don't, they have about ten per cent and I think it shows in their behaviour.

> In the car his sister wanted some chocolate, and I have to say

*they can only have some if they feed Tim as well. You just have to
say 'no' to all of them unless they feed him. And he bites their
fingers – they don't really want to feed him … or we have to wait
until he falls asleep. It seems very mean, really.*

Success depends on parents thinking and planning ahead, and being
well organised and often well resourced. Strategies include making
time and space for each child to have some undivided attention and to
enjoy their own preferred activities, away from the limitations
imposed by a brother or sister's special needs. But this itself imposes
an extra burden on parents and, once again, depends on someone else
being available to look after the child with special needs:

*They both like going swimming and I go every other Friday with
them because I have somebody who comes to look after Tim
when he gets home from school. He's quite miffed that he
doesn't go swimming when the girls do, but when you do things
with all of them it centres round Tim and I just think the girls need
space. So that's their space now, once a fortnight.*

*I think for Sean [Aidan's younger brother] in a way it stops him
being invited back sometimes because Aidan gets on with lots of
children, especially Sean's friends. Sometimes they're thought of
as a pair, rather than just Aidan or just Sean. So I think whereas
someone might quite like to have one child back, they're not
necessarily going to be able to cope with two, whether they've
got a handicap or not. So now I manage to see that they're not
[regarded as] an actual pair – Sean can come on his own and I'll
take Aidan somewhere else.*

Integrated activities can provide a solution by bringing siblings
together in a setting where neither is disadvantaged for the sake of
the other and interests can be shared in a valuable way. However,
very few families mentioned that their children had taken part in
such groups:

*The [special] school had their holiday club. William [brother
without special needs] and his friends went along and they
absolutely loved it. And they also went to one to do with their
school, and when I asked them which one they liked best, they*

said the special school. William loved it and can't wait to go to the next one.

How siblings react to a brother or sister with disabilities varies according to personality, and sometimes also according to their age and position in the family. Parents have to find ways of helping their children to understand the disability and deal with the situation in a way that suits their children's age and understanding. The attitudes of the rest of the community – friends, relations, school, neighbourhood and the general public – have a significant effect on siblings' attitudes to disability and on their own self-esteem.

We said to him [brother], *'What do you think's the matter with Carly?' and he just says that she's ill. Because he's too young to really understand it himself. So we thought we'll leave it until he knows enough to understand that she's actually not ill as such, but she's not going to be the same as other boys and girls until she's a lot older.*

The oldest son, it affected him more when I had Rosie because he wasn't too sure how she was going to be, what she was going to look like? Robert's had to learn to say to people, 'Oh, I've got a sister with Down's Syndrome,' and then they'll say, 'Oh, I've got a brother who can't hear, or a cousin who...'. That way he's realised that there are other people who have problems. But he'll always say to a new friend after a bit, 'I have a sister with Downs Syndrome,' so they know. Whereas for his younger brother [also a teenager] *it was no problem. He wasn't bothered in the slightest. She was just his sister, she was just Rosie.*

Several parents commented that the experience of integrated schooling makes a difference to other children's perceptions of disability and their ability to respond positively:

Natasha [Mark's younger sister] *and her friends find Mark easier to cope with. Somehow they can get their brains around the fact that Mark is Mark. Whether it's the fact that all Natasha's friends have been to their shared school, so they're familiar with Mark from school. I think Leon* [Mark's older brother] *worries about*

*having friends around. But the friend that he selects copes with it
quite well ... Their experience of Mark is very different from their
school experience, because the school that he and Leon went to
didn't have much in the way of special needs provision.*

*I really do feel that to have children with special needs in
[mainstream] schools is a great help to other children. Rupert, who
is 26, had a boy with Down's Syndrome in his class and they are
still friendly and in touch with each other. Rupert is very friendly
and relaxed with any person with any special needs, and yet my
other son – who didn't have a child with special needs in his class –
isn't at ease. He's lovely with Paul* [younger brother with disability]
*because Paul is his brother and he adores him, but outside the
family he isn't comfortable with special needs children or people.*

How far children want, or are able, to include a brother or sister
with special needs also varies. The nature of the disability can affect
the activities and pastimes that can be shared:

*If asked, Mark's siblings will include him, but generally it has to be
a physical activity such as cycling or skateboarding. They will take
him to the park, but I couldn't let him go for very long. Natasha,
his younger sister, is much more likely to include him. Leon, his
older brother, less so. Leon has to be asked.*

I don't think Carl [older brother] *even likes Joseph any more.
Joseph is so awful – he goes into Carl's room and wrecks
everything.*

Experience from the London Community Project run by The Children's Society shows that, certainly in the recent past, disabled and
non-disabled siblings are likely to have had dissimilar preschool
experience and to have been educated separately. This leads to
entirely separate friendship groups and out-of-school experiences,
opportunities and interests. Thus, in adolescence, the disabled child
may well never have had many of the experiences that form the basis
of his or her siblings' lives – with the result that they have little in
common on which to build a relationship. If the disabled child has
gone away to residential school or respite care, they may not even
have day-to-day living in common.

SUMMARY

It is vital that the efforts of families with a disabled child are under-pinned by regular respite care, organised either formally or informally, to enable parents to focus on their own lives and the needs of other family members. Finding good, reliable care was a problem for all families and not everyone could rely on help from the extended family or friends. Those parents who had access to care organised by volun-tary or statutory agencies usually spoke positively of it. However, along with specialist services provided for the child, such support sys-tems are often inflexible and fail to take account of the family as a whole. Interruptions to services, long waits, badly-planned access and poor facilities increase the stress and inconvenience already experi-enced by families.

In addition, assessments and therapeutic sessions can easily become all-consuming, imposing further strain on families and the disabled child. Guilt was a commonly-expressed theme here, with parents feel-ing they could never do enough for their child. The disproportionate level of attention that needs to be focused on the disabled child is usually at the expense of other siblings, creating a very difficult situation for parents to manage. However, it was evident that brothers and sisters also provide some of the best opportunities for including the disabled sibling in the wider world and thus extending his or her experiences.

CHAPTER 4

Living in the real world

The main part of the study examined how far parents are able to include their children with disabilities in all the different aspects of everyday life. Everyday life extends beyond the things we enjoy doing – joining clubs, meeting friends and family socially. It includes those activities, such as shopping, that are part of the ordinary family routine and others that are essential to meet the child's everyday needs – a child with disabilities still has to go to the hairdresser or buy new shoes.

FRIENDSHIPS

The first friends of young children are always other children their parents know – cousins and other relatives, the children of friends and neighbours. They may not be 'friends' as such, just children they spend time with and are expected to play with. As children grow, and go first to preschool groups and then to school, they develop friendships of their own choosing with some children from the many they meet. They also make friends spontaneously, perhaps for just an hour or so, with children they meet playing in the street or in parks, on the beach, at the pool, on holiday, etc.

How far can children with special needs be included in these friendship networks, for friends are a very important element of feeling included, learning to socialise and avoiding isolation and loneliness? Perhaps more than in any other area discussed in this report, the nature and degree of the disability concerned affects the extent to which friendships can develop. Children with profound and multiple disabilities, or children with communication disorders, are most likely to be sidelined when it comes to proper friendships:

*Because of his problems he doesn't really understand. It takes a
long time for him to recognise someone ... He hasn't got friends
as kids turn round and say, 'Oh, can John come?'. Gregory hasn't
got friends like that. He hasn't got any friends, really. That sounds
awful, doesn't it?*

*He wants to interact now, but he doesn't know how to. He's
'learnt' to play. I've had children round here, they're happy to play
a particular game for five or ten minutes, then they want to stop
and play something else. And James can't understand that. He
gets extremely upset or annoyed because they don't want to
continue playing. It's never a really nice relaxing time. There's
always a problem with his autistic side.*

By contrast, parents of children whose disabilities do not significantly impair their social functioning report the huge importance their
children attach to friendships. The ability to make and keep friends
contributes a great deal to their enjoyment of life and to their feelings
of autonomy:

*I think his special friend is Toby, who likes fighting. You know, he's
a normal little boy, really, he likes fighting and messing around.*

*She loves children coming here, she absolutely loves it. She's very
social like that, loves her little girlfriend coming round for tea.*

*He's a typical little boy, he's in love with a little girl. He's got all the
emotions of a normal child.*

Obstacles to forming friendships

Even children who very much want to socialise and can make their
feelings known find many obstacles in the way of forming friendships.
Young children with busy therapeutic schedules have little opportunity
for ordinary socialising. Although they may meet other children at hos-
pitals, clinics and so on, friendships are not possible unless the parents
are willing to work at extending the relationship:

*The reason I really want to get her into school is so that she's
going to be with the same people day in, day out, she's going to
get to recognise them, she's going to get friends. Whereas now,*

*with all the different activities I have to do, she doesn't know who
anybody is. She only sees them for an hour or so.*

The situation is the same at special schools, where children tend to
come from different neighbourhoods and would not meet naturally
outside school. Being taken to and from school on special transport
means that there are no opportunities for spontaneous 'school gate'
social arrangements. Parents do not meet every day at school and so
have no opportunity to get to know each other and carry out the informal 'vetting' that often happens before they allow a child to go off into
someone else's care:

*What happens in special schools is that the children tend to live
so far from the school. It's okay having children round when they
live round the corner and you can just nip them home, but when
it's an hour round trip you tend to think twice about it.*

*He has one friend at the school – if he wants to go to his house
it's really difficult because they're not allowed to go in each
other's taxis. So I have to actually go and meet him and take him
to this friend's house. It's really difficult.*

Parents also commented that the small size of classes in special
schools, although ideal educationally, does not provide as wide a social
circle as a larger class in a mainstream school. Parents find that special
schools place little emphasis on developing wider social networks:

*He is invited to birthday parties, but not as many – because of his
arthritis, because he's only in a class of nine. Whereas if he didn't
have arthritis and was in a mainstream school, he'd be in a class
of thirty, which means more parties and more everything.*

I recognise he needs a special environment [but] *I wish the school
he went to was bigger. Because he only has his everyday life with
these eight or nine children with a couple of years' age span and
multiple problems ... okay, he's got* [problems] *too, but he needs
something else ... His creative abilities are not impaired at all, nor
his ability to sing, and he's learning the drums. He's outgoing, but
the difficulty comes when he wants to join in with other kids
because he's at such a small special school that there's no other
kids doing that sort of thing.*

Even when parents do all they can to encourage friendships and extend invitations, often these are not reciprocated:

[When] *she went to this group, she had two birthday parties and children from* [the group] *came here to the house, but there was never any return invitation.*

Parents understand that there can be good reasons for the lack of invitations for their child and for the failure to accept their own invitations. Other families may feel cautious about their ability to meet the child's special needs, especially if they differ from their own child's. Other factors are time, distance and the need for parents to have enough energy:

Aidan gets invited to birthday parties and things like that, but he's never been particularly [invited] *in a spontaneous way like, 'Would you like to come back this afternoon? Come to tea? Come to my house?'. It would be more arranged. The mother's got to gear herself up, I suppose.*

We don't see any of his friends from school at home here, although on the annual event we have on Tim's birthday we invite the school, but so far only one of his friends ever comes for that. Maybe it's a problem with the distance. Maybe the parents of disabled children don't feel they can take their children to a strange party. I don't know.

However, parents are delighted when their child is invited to play with other children and regard this little step into the social world as very important:

Katy went to a party a couple of weeks ago, which I was really pleased about because she was invited – somebody from nursery invited her!

WHOSE FRIENDS?

In many cases a disabled child's social circle is based on the extended family rather than on the friends he or she has selected. This is partly because opportunities for friendship are limited, as discussed above. Another important reason is that, just as the development of children with disabilities is at a younger level than their chronological age, so their social networks are similar to those of very young children:

One thing that's totally different for Catherine, her birthday parties tend to be our parents and her godparents and not young children, because she hasn't really got friends as such.

He's got quite a few cousins, so I tend to have an open house [for his birthday] and everybody turns up in the afternoon – nans, granddads, aunties and cousins – and it's just full house for Gregory.

Parents also find that, while children with disabilities might well be included as part of a 'family package' invitation, they do not get invitations in their own right. This, they feel, is better than nothing and means that their child is part way to having a social network of his or her own. However, it is not quite the same as their other children experienced:

I think we've still got to see if Georgia gets invited round to see people on her own ... The most that happens is that Georgia gets invited along with William [brother], which is nice. William's friends like her, so they go along together and she plays with the boys.

INTEGRATED PLAY

Parents' instincts are to give their children as wide a range of social opportunities as possible that are appropriate to their child's particular needs:

We just felt we wanted her to be with other children in situations and she coped quite well. We wanted her to have access to all children and be friends with all sorts of children.

He used to go to a playgroup which catered for special needs and it was very good because they had able-bodied children. He benefited from that because it enabled him to socialise with a bunch of children ... We've always felt that this was necessary for his own intellectual development and social development.

The reality of integrated play has advantages and disadvantages. Sometimes it has to be 'managed' by the parents in order to make it work well for all concerned:

You would go and visit a group of friends and they would tell their children, 'You must be a little bit careful with Nicholas because of his having a walking stick.' If you pushed him, he would fall over. Now, you just have to be a bit careful that Nicholas doesn't go round and whack one of the others. He is now the leader of the play because he missed out, he was never a toddler – he's now making up for it.

The parameters of his social life I don't think are different to other children's social life, but I think you are aware that he does need more attention, that he's less trustworthy with things, you have to be on guard and you have to be quite clear that the people he's with understand that.

Helping their children to join in ordinary social activities can sometimes be very taxing for parents. Besides the physical and emotional toll, they see at first hand that their children miss out on some vital parts of the fun and pleasure. One parent of a child with profound, multiple disabilities commented:

She gets invited to a lot [of parties]. *I must admit I don't often take her – basically because I think she'd enjoy it for a little while, but I would just end up holding her. If there are too many children around, I can't lie her on the floor because she gets trodden on or kicked. She can't eat any of the food or drink the Coke. She can't play any of the games. So I tend not to take her. I'd like to be able to. I feel I should make more of an effort so that she would get used to other children, but it's just too much for me.*

Sometimes, the behaviour of other children can upset the disabled child. On other occasions, parents realise that their child is being left out, even though he or she remains unaware:

When we went to the pier, my nephew and this other boy ran off together and left Joseph, ran off holding hands, and Joseph was left standing there. That upset me, annoyed me a bit. My nephew knew what he was doing, and they had a little whisper together and decided to leave Joseph.

However, children do learn how to behave in order to include a child with disabilities. If all the children involved have a degree of choice, so that the friendship becomes real and not just something expected, these unfortunate incidents may happen less often:

> *I've got a friend who has a little boy – he loves Chloe. I know she recognises him: she smiles when she hears his voice and he is really gentle with her. He has got to know her and knows how to be with her. She's better on a one-to-one with other children rather than with lots of children.*

> *Children are remarkable, absolutely remarkable, and there's never been a problem with how they are towards her. My niece – she's eight – is particularly good, she'll really include Lottie in the games they're playing. Like if they're playing cards then Lottie will have some cards to play with.*

Parents may feel that their child is more included when he or she is not the only one with special needs. True friendship is based on having things in common with other people and feeling comfortable with them. Sometimes, it is natural to choose friends who also have special needs, especially since the gap between the interests and needs of disabled and non-disabled children can widen as they grow older. Children with disabilities may like to have some friends who have had similar experiences. In an ideal world, children would have a social circle broad enough for them to find compatible companions, both disabled and non-disabled, to fulfil all the various roles that friends can play:

> *The best thing about Christina going to boarding school is that for the first time in her life she has got some friends. And that was one of the most important things for me, that she should be with other children all on the same sort of wavelength as her who would accept her for herself.*

> *It's lovely to see her with her friends at school. There must be bad times but I don't see them. There are fewer Down's children at [her special school]. They seem to be going to MLD [Moderate Learning Difficulties] schools, and some to normal schools, and I can see why parents are wanting it, but in a way you want them to have more of the children like them together so that they can have a larger friendship group.*

As with many aspects of getting a child with special needs included, successful friendship networks depend on parental intercession and forward planning, plus physical effort to make things work well:

She's often said at weekends, 'Are my friends coming too?'. And maybe we should make more effort to take one of her friends. It's just that you have to plan these things in advance.

We take John to all the children's birthday parties and make sure that when they're all sitting down, he's sitting at the table, probably on my lap, and I just get him as involved as possible ... try to be as normal as possible, just join in. And he really loves it, he loves being round other children. He loves the noise, loves being roughed about.

OUT AND ABOUT

Getting out of the house – to visit friends and family, to take part in groups and leisure pursuits outside the home, and in everyday activities such as shopping – is essential to achieving inclusion. With young children, many of these trips can be difficult enough even if they do not have special needs, but as children grow up and become more independent the trips come to involve much less effort and organisation. That said, in recent years parental concerns about children's personal safety, and the danger of heavier traffic, have restricted the independence of all young children and have led to increased supervision. Almost all parents expect to be heavily involved in transporting and supervising children outside the home.

While the parents in this report acknowledged that it is hard to get around with very young children who are able-bodied, they felt that their child's special needs make the situation even more difficult. Their problems would continue when non-disabled children have grown more independent. Developing independence itself can bring further problems (see also Chapter 5):

The care aspect became most difficult when he was eleven or twelve, when other people's children started being able to get the bus into town on their own or with a friend and started to be more independent. They could go to school on their own, and at that stage he was absolutely nowhere near ready to do that, and there was such a rift. But now at thirteen and a half he's actually got the bus into town on his own, got what he wanted and got back. I thought, 'Well, this is a breakthrough, good.' He can only do that because he'd done it with his friends. I noticed he went with his friends three or four times before he made that one trip to the one shop and came back. How much do you let them go? That's the problem for me, really.

TRANSPORT

The first essential seems to be a car, though not everyone has one. This parent spoke for many:

We have our own car. We'd be absolutely lost without it. I know people who haven't got cars in our situation and it is really hard for them. It limits what you can do for your child.

Public transport presents many problems for children with disabilities and their families, enough to deter some completely. Managing both children and equipment is difficult or downright impossible without assistance from staff or fellow passengers. Some families develop a thick-skinned approach to getting their needs met:

I did [use public transport] *once, but it was a nightmare. You can't use public transport because you can't hold a child and get on a bus, and have a pushchair and pay your bus fare, it's just an impossible job on your own.*

We take the double buggy on the train, that's quite easy to do. I make sure they're both strapped in and the guard helps me on the train. The train can't go because I open the door and they have to wait!

PUSHCHAIRS

Difficulties that apply to all young children, such as the need for pushchairs and pushchair-friendly environments, continue for much longer when a child's walking is delayed or a wheelchair has to be used after the buggy has been outgrown. Children with behaviour difficulties may need a pushchair for much longer because, although they can walk, they may not always co-operate; a pushchair is a useful fall-back strategy to enable them to get to their destination. Others need a pushchair because they tire easily or have other physical problems:

He needs a pushchair even though he can walk because if he walks too far, then his legs are quite stiff the next day. So it's better for him to walk a little way and then put him in the pushchair.

The thing that makes me feel most excluded is the physical problems. For anybody who has a disablement – and any mother who's got a child in a buggy is disabled – as soon as you go out, you're excluded. It doesn't need to be like that for anybody.

Equipment can be borrowed, but this may create further anxieties:

This buggy I've got is not mine. It's the property of the physiotherapy department ... so I'm more careful with this than you would be with your own. And without it, I'd be really stuck anyway, so I can't afford to lose it because it would stop me doing everything. If I've not got the car, I've taken the buggy and walked to the shops ... but they don't have buggy places, places where you can put your buggy and pay 20p to have it safeguarded – so I tend to go round with a basket and the buggy. I can't understand how they haven't developed a trolley that can either go in front of a wheelchair, or in front of or behind a buggy.

Growing children bring additional problems:

Taking the double buggy isn't all that easy because of the shop doorways and things like that. Because he's bigger, he's very heavy in it.

When he was little I could actually carry him in his seat if it was for a short distance, but I can't now.

SUITABLE FOR DISABLED PEOPLE?

Some environments that claim to be designed to help people with disabilities are in reality poorly planned and are neither child-friendly nor disabled-friendly. Others suffer from poor management:

When I had to go and get his Orange Badge for the car – his disabled badge – there are steps all the way up there. It's pathetic – all these people in their wheelchairs and pushchairs are at the bottom and you can't get in there.

I get so angry when people park in disabled bays when they're not supposed to. I've got some stickers and I stick them on people's windscreens. Once we went to the supermarket and Laura was with us – there were people in the disabled bays and I parked my car in an awkward spot and the manager removed it! And I told him why I had parked there. Now he patrols the car park and sends cars away if they haven't got the Orange Badge.

Better planning and management of public environments to create genuine access for disabled people would be a real improvement. Better information would also allow families to plan more successfully:

It would be good to have a brochure of what's available in your area with wheelchair access – what's suitable, what's really suitable for the disabled.

SHOPPING

Shopping is such a regular aspect of family life that all parents have to try to incorporate their child in the routine. For some children and young people, shopping is an enjoyable and stimulating activity (as the young people themselves report in Chapter 2). Supermarket shopping is easy for families who have managed to find suitable equipment:

Shopping? Now it's easy, it's great. He enjoys it, we love shopping now. He can sit in a [chain name] supermarket trolley, he can't sit in anyone else's trolley. You get different trolleys for various different needs and they're great.

In the big supermarkets, the new trolleys have got double seats [for babies and children], so that makes it a lot easier.

However, the regular family shop can cause familiar difficulties. Some children find the supermarket environment distressing or alarming and the equipment unsuitable. Although in recent years the large supermarket chains have done a great deal to improve the design and variety of trolleys available to meet the needs of shoppers with young children, they still have some way to go for both children and adults with disabilities. Many parents, particularly of preschool children, have to use precious respite care or rely on a family member to come with them or to shop for them – another aspect of life that is more complicated for families with a disabled child:

> We tried it [supermarket shopping] *once with John – that was enough! I thought he'd like all the noise because he loves noise. I thought he'd go to sleep and he didn't. He just went totally stiff ... screamed. I got as far as the second alley, I thought, 'No', and we went home. So now we either do it on a Friday on a* [respite] *day, which isn't ideal, or one of us will go while the other has John.*

> *They have trolleys now with the seat fitted for babies, but it's rock hard. If it had something soft in it, she might sit a bit better. It's just got one strap that comes up between her legs. It's not safe enough for her. She just screams.*

OTHER OBSTACLES

Going out in public places for children whose behaviour is unpredictable or difficult to manage can be problematic. The problems can affect not just the child's enjoyment of the outing, but that of the whole family and also the child's own safety:

> *I lose him everywhere. I do panic about it. People might think it is irresponsible of me to let go, but I've only got to let go of his wrist for a second to pay for something or take my change. It's awful, you let go for a second, even to turn around and change your grip, and he's gone.*

> *It's more than just embarrassment. If he made a very loud train noise you would just think, 'Oh, I wish he wouldn't do that', but if he starts to lie down to do a 'whirly' on the floor, there are obviously difficulties in that people might want to get past.*

Careful planning and timing are necessary for trips with children with severe and complex difficulties:

> *It does require some effort. If we're going out for a walk, it's not a two-minute job to get Catherine out. We've got to allow for her being catheterised, that restricts you an awful lot. There's just nowhere to*

do that sort of thing in public. That works out at mealtimes, so it makes it difficult for us to be able to have a meal out as well.

We can't just all get up and go, we've got to think of Joanne's tea, Joanne needs changing, is Joanne tired? Joanne can fit when she's tired so basically we have a certain few hours in the day when we can go out with her, which is quite a tie.

LEISURE ACTIVITIES

Access to mainstream leisure activities of all sorts helps children with disabilities to be part of their community; to meet other children and widen their experiences. Some leisure activities – such as swimming or going to the park – also allow families with a disabled child to feel that they can do things together, just like other families.

Playgroups and swimming lessons are the most popular activities. Others include holiday playschemes, dance classes, Girls' Brigade, Cubs, Beavers, gym club and arts projects.

ORGANISED GROUPS

For some parents, 'joining in' means enabling their child to have the same sort of experiences as other children of about the same age. Going to mainstream groups also allows children with special needs to become 'just children', without the activity's specific therapeutic benefits taking priority. Small things that make a child with disabilities feel just like other children are very important:

She seems to enjoy [the Opportunity Playgroup], *in fact she gets quite excited on the mornings when she goes, and it's nice because she comes home with paintings and all the things that ordinary children come home with. Most of the things in the playgroup are just things that the other kids can do and so Chloe just joins in, if and how she can, obviously with help.*

She used to go to ballet classes, which was lovely. Katy loved it ... Sometimes she would go off and do her own thing, but other children would pull her back into the right place and try and show her what she was supposed to do. I found it very encouraging that little children could just accept her.

For many children, the main advantage of an integrated preschool play setting is the opportunity to widen their circle of friends. Often it represents their first chance ever to meet and mix with other children without disabilities. Joining in local activities also enables children and their families to make neighbourhood contacts, which for young families are a very important part of developing a supportive social network:

We saw him getting so much from the playgroup, where other children simply accepted him as just another person, as a child sat there quietly rather than a disabled child. He got more from that social group than he does probably from his social group [in a special school] *now.*

With Katy going to playgroup [some miles away] *it wasn't easy to build up relationships, whereas the playgroup that Steven will be going to is only just down the road, so there will be more people locally who will be going there, so maybe we will meet more people that way.* [Both children have special needs.]

We get Playlink, it goes all over the whole of [our neighbourhood] *and we go out on trips to the farm, and to the jamborina the other week, and we're getting included in things like that.*

Joining in with specific activities allows children with disabilities to develop their own skills and interests, and to begin to discover how to make choices about what they want to do. It can also help children and young people to expand their horizons beyond what their immediate family can provide:

She does swimming classes with ordinary children. I went with her for the first two sessions and pushed her in the right direction. She now goes on her own with no problems at all. She loves her swimming, she really does.

It's an arts project and there's quite a lot of adults involved, professional adults, and they'll make puppets. He can thrive in this environment. It'll be wonderful because if he can find a niche where his disability isn't getting in the way, he can be wonderful, he can act brilliantly. If he's confident, he's really confident and very bubbly.

He was invited on holiday with his friend's family and this was wonderful. He even attempted windsurfing. Between the father of this family and the instructor, they worked out how he could do it and he just did it and really enjoyed it. I'm very lucky to have friends like that because if I didn't, he would miss out on that kind of fuss-free, worry-free environment that somebody else can provide.

A number of parents said that their ideal would be a properly planned, integrated group, although these are all too rare. Successful integrated activities also allow siblings to join in and should be able to offer as much to non-disabled children as to disabled children, taking into account the needs of the children involved. In such activities, which should have sufficient staff to offer appropriate support for children to participate, the focus is on play. Art, craft, drama, music and so on are so designed to include and interest all the children present:

I've enrolled Clare for this integrated playscheme. It sounds like the answer to all my prayers. I've never particularly wanted her to go to the holiday special needs playscheme because I felt that during the holidays it's been good for her to be with the family, to be with ordinary kids rather than just special needs children all the time. I feel they're [the integrated playscheme] all geared up for Clare.

However, some parents find that mixed or 'mainstream' activities are not the most enjoyable way for their child to experience similar things to other children. Sometimes their needs are not targeted appropriately, or the needs of different disabled children are too dissimilar. On occasions, discrimination makes the experience uncomfortable or distressing:

He went on an outing with his friend, who's able-bodied, to this activity centre. The centre was used to disabled kids, that wasn't the problem. The problem was that the other kids teased him and called him names and started pointing at his hands. And because this was a day's outing, he wasn't with adults who knew him, it wasn't dealt with, and he came back very depressed and said, 'I'm not going on anything like that ever again.' Now he seems to have lost a bit of confidence in going out in the world, but it's really important that he does.

Parks and swimming pools are the most popular places for outings. Some parents find the facilities available there useful and reasonably well suited to their child's needs:

The good thing about swimming is that people don't do a lot of talking. She doesn't stand out too much and there's a lot of noise to cover up any strange noises she was making. So she could be integrated quite well in swimming.

He loves going to parks. He sits on my knee on the swings and laughs his head off when I swing backwards and forwards.

However, poor facilities deter some parents. Play equipment is frequently unsuitable for children with disabilities and the temperature in swimming pools is often too low. Another criticism is of poor planning and design, a problem magnified by the fact that parents with a disabled child have to cope with a family-unfriendly environment for far longer than other parents:

We can't really go to the park. She can't go on the swings because she can't hold her head up. She can't come down the slide – she can't do anything. I have tried. I've taken towels and tried to prop her up, but she doesn't like it. I go there anyway and sit with her so that she can see all the other children. That was the whole reason we moved here – the park just round the corner. I thought it was going to be lovely. I thought, 'I'll take my little girl over the park'.

Nicholas couldn't have gone to [the public swimming pool] *because the water would have been too cold. We went away on holiday and Nicholas went swimming in the ordinary pool, and every time he came out of the pool we had to put him in the jacuzzi to warm him up because his joints start to seize.*

Public places such as parks, where most children have no difficulty using the facilities provided, make some parents feel self-conscious and very aware of their child's disabilities. Disabled children themselves are often aware of the limits their disability imposes. In these circumstances, children need extra effort from their parents to enable them to join in:

*He likes to go to the park – he can go on the swings – but I
choose to go when it's quiet. I feel in a way it's torturing him
because he sees all these kids in the sandpit, and if I'm not
feeling up to it then I will just sit there and he'll just watch. He's
quite happy watching, but if he wants to get in there, if he's
feeling active, it's hard work, it's really hard work.*

OBSTACLES TO JOINING IN

Being included means more than just turning up at activities designed
for non-disabled people and being expected to join in as best as one
can. Joining in means becoming actively involved, with whatever help
and support is needed to achieve that. This can involve having an ancil-
lary helper at a playgroup, or providing aids to ensure that a child can
reach table height or move around. Creative thinking, good communication between parents and carers, and thoughtful forward planning are
all essential. In some cases, only small adjustments may be required; in
others a major reorganisation and extra funding. Above all, attitudes
may have to change so as to prevent deliberate or tacit exclusion:

*She was in the creche and she was fine. They were doing an
Easter egg hunt and [the organisers] brought her back to me
because she can't walk, and they said, 'You'll have to look after
her. We're all going off now.' That sort of thing really makes me
angry because I thought somebody should have carried her, or
they should have told me to bring the buggy and she could have
been wheeled round. She's only little and it was only round the
playground, not like they were going miles.*

*They had paintboards and everyone was painting, and Chloe didn't
do any painting or anything. I thought that's easy, all she has to do
is sit on someone's lap and they could put a paintbrush in her
hand and just help her guide it. It was so easy, but they didn't
bother. Things like that aren't difficult to do and she enjoys them.*

Most crucial of all is the need for everyone involved in running children's groups and activities to gain a better understanding of disability,
and of the expectations appropriate for children with disabilities. Lack
of understanding can lead to children not being included in a way that
works successfully:

Unfortunately [the playgroup's] *expectations of a child with Down's Syndrome are much lower and they don't expect him to be able to do a form-board, and a child that's bored – any child that's bored – is naughty.*

She attends Sunday school, where she's in a completely mixed setting. We just ask the staff to treat her as they do the other children, but just to be a little wary of how tired she gets and if she's getting stiff. When she's fit and well, she's just one of the group, but there are some people who generally expect her to underperform, so that's what she does, and when they're on duty she shifts to that pattern. I think children are very good at changing their behaviour to the [expectations] *around them.*

I suppose he could mix more with other children. It's okay him mixing as long as whoever is in charge does involve him. He spent ten months with a nursery, but we found we'd be going in and John was just lying on the floor and no one was with him. It didn't always happen, but he was starting to get left out.

Parents may feel tentative about exploring the possibilities of children joining in mainstream leisure activities because of the extra efforts that they know the organisers would have to make. Sometimes, the reactions of those in charge do little to make parents feel confident about asking. However, in other cases, once parents have established good communication with the group leaders, the situation can be managed successfully:

At Sunday school she went to the baby section when she was very young. But we just felt she needed watching so much. We couldn't expect someone to look after her as well as teach when there were terrific numbers in the Sunday school anyway, unless we were willing to be with her the whole time. We felt we hadn't the time to be in church and attend Sunday school with her as well, so she comes with us to church, but she doesn't get the teaching at a childlike level.

She used to go to ballet classes. When I approached the teacher, she was a bit wary.

Anything she wants to do, we'll put her into it and see how she

*gets on and if she enjoys it, or if we think it's benefiting her. We
take the view that you try and set targets which are achievable.
Also, you have to bear in mind the teachers because you can't
allow her to disrupt the group and disrupt the other children. And
we're quite sensitive to the teachers – we're asking if things are
going okay or if there's a problem, and we do talk to them about
that.*

For preschool children, a busy timetable of therapeutic input and
assessments makes it hard to find the time and energy for other
activities. This applies to the child, and also to the parent who has to
take and collect their child and perhaps also support him or her
during the activity. Some school-age children who have long days
travelling to special school and home again also lack spare time and
energy:

*For five days a week we're not mixing, we're in the special side
doing all the special things for John. So I wouldn't say we're really
included in the community, we're on the other side of things.*

He does have long days, he [four-year-old] *leaves here at ten past
eight and the earliest he gets back is ten past four. He goes five
days a week. At the end of the day, all he wants to do is have his
tea and sit and watch telly, which I think is quite reasonable after a
day that long.*

FAMILY ACTIVITIES

Parents described a wide range of successful family activities and outings enthusiastically. Including a disabled child in a range of family
activities is good not only for him or her, but for the family as a whole.
Here is the chance to relax, to choose manageable things that children
and families like doing and meet, as far as possible, everyone's needs
and wishes.

*We go everywhere. We try to take Laura to everything that we go
to, but we bear in mind that she's in a wheelchair. So the beach is
really out because you can't take her chair on the sand. We take
her on the pier, we've taken her fishing. When we go on holiday,
she goes on the fairground rides with her dad. She's been*

swimming, to restaurants, anything. Most of the time there isn't a problem with her chair.

A lot of people would never contemplate climbing up the stairs to the top of Bodiam Castle, but to me, if the other children are doing it, Tim does it also.

We go into the woods a lot, which is why I made the special chair with a longer wheelbase than an ordinary wheelchair with small wheels, and it's steerable. I felt I had to make something like that because I couldn't take the wheelchair into places where other children would want to go.

Visiting National Trust and similar properties is popular, perhaps because they have something for everyone and also endeavour to provide well-planned and well-signed disabled access. Families also enjoy informal events, where their disabled child can be included without any pressure:

We go to National Trust properties and we'll go and walk around houses, she likes doing that. We can do things like that. We can walk around lovely gardens, it's very nice – not too many people so she can walk by herself.

We go to cricket and it's brilliant. Living in the village, everybody knows Catherine and they all come up and talk to her, which is lovely. They don't ignore her at all. They all play together and then we'll go on the swings. They all make an effort to make sure she's included.

The best thing to do really is to go round someone's house, friends' and relatives' or whatever, because I can take everything with me and there is no problem.

However, keeping everyone happy can mean juggling different needs, which is not always easy as these change as children grow up. What individual families manage to do depends on careful and imaginative planning, and on how resourceful they are feeling. A stressed and overtaxed family will not be able to provide so many opportunities for inclusion. The child's busy schedule and specific needs create additional limitations:

It's very hard to have everyone happy and it's things like the beach that they all still like.

The main thing is that we can't go out in the country and walk, we can't walk on the Downs. We'd like to do that. We really have to be somewhere where there's pavement and we can push the pushchair.

We get so little time now because his hospital's here and his group's there, but any time we get together we make sure we go swimming or go to the park, or do something Lee's really going to enjoy.

Here one parent speaks for many:

It would be lovely to get up and go, at any time of day, to any event.

EATING OUT

Many families enjoy eating out these days – there are cafes and restaurants suitable for all budgets and far more of them welcome children than in the past. Some families with a disabled child find that going out for a meal is an enjoyable activity suitable for the whole family. Despite possible problems, it symbolises inclusion and holds greater potential for enjoyment than many other activities:

[Our fourteen-year-old's] eating skills have certainly improved and she loves it, she's very independent. As she says, 'I like to do it myself.' So we often eat out with the children and she copes very well. They like to go to restaurants and have a coffee and watch everybody.

I've always taken Christina to restaurants ever since she was very small. She's actually better behaved than a lot of six-year-old children who aren't used to being in restaurants.

Other families are less than happy about the experience. Worries about behaviour are one reason for not eating out together. A general feeling of high expectations about children 'behaving themselves' in places such as restaurants makes parents feel uncomfortable. One parent said: 'I don't think it matters whether they are children or special needs children, they are just not accepted.' The problem can be magnified with a child with a learning disability, who is not necessarily able to behave in a way onlookers deem suitable for his or her age and size. Some parents feel that their child's behaviour will be judged harshly and that other people will not make allowances for their special needs:

> We tend not to go into restaurants with Lee just in case he starts to kick up a stink, because people just don't like badly-behaved children.

> She'll whinge continually so it's difficult to try and eat your own food as well as keep her quiet. You know what people are like when you're out and you've got a child whinging. We just take sandwiches or come home and have something to eat, or we get [food] and eat it in the car. It's easier then.

Some restaurants are very helpful and accommodate special requirements. In others, parents find it difficult to get their child's needs met, often because of a failure to understand the situation:

> Restaurants we most often go to – they know that when I say, 'Can I have some garlic bread and some Coke extremely quickly?' they know I mean extremely quickly!

> They actually seat us away from all the others because it feels better, because of Joanne's feeding. Everyone stares when I feed her because she dribbles and she takes a long time to feed. It's not that you're ashamed of her when you sit away [from other people], but I would rather be in a corner so that I can be left on my own. So we do find we go to certain places to eat because it's comfortable and they know us.

HOLIDAYS

The aim of going on holiday is for everyone to enjoy themselves, relax and have a much-needed break. However, the majority of parents who manage to get away as a family find that they cannot achieve this, often because the difficulties encountered at home are magnified in unfamiliar surroundings. These include the lack of the equipment and facilities they are used to at home, the absence of familiar people to give support and surroundings that are unsuitable for the needs of their child:

It was a total disaster! It's much harder work than staying at home. We came back more exhausted than before we went.

We just needed to get away so we went to a caravan in the Lake District, which was familiar ground to us. But she was just so ill, the effort that it had taken to pack everything up and to travel was completely wasted. It was worse having got there – being in a place that you love – to have that just outside the caravan door and not being able to get out there, but just to have to look after her.

Some families found it difficult to find suitable accommodation:

We've been looking at hotels that said we'd be catered for. The first priority [when looking] in the brochure is the facilities for the disabled, so every one [we've chosen] has got disabled facilities and they welcome children. The problem I've had is that their family rooms are not on the ground floor, so they're not suitable for disabled people. People seem to think that disabled people only come in pairs and they're old. They get the ground floor rooms. At the moment, I haven't found anything at all so we're stuck.

We had a cheap holiday out of season at [a holiday camp]. There was a creche – they're meant to accommodate handicapped children – and I took her along. Because she escaped once, they said they wouldn't have her. In a way that was taking away the offer that they make in their information and I find that quite hard. It was the way it was done. I was made to feel I had produced a monster, not a person, and that was hurtful.

However, holidays abroad can prove to be a positive and inclusive experience:

It's quite nice when we go on holiday in a foreign country because they don't realise. They talk to Clare. Because they don't speak English, they don't realise there's so much of a problem.

We went to France with her when she was about two and they were just marvellous. You'd feel welcomed as a family. I don't feel as relaxed here as I did in France.

SUMMARY

Friendships for children with disabilities are vitally important for their happiness, autonomy and development, but it must be recognised that genuine friendship involves choice from both sides. Many parents felt that special schooling environments limited the child's social circle and restricted opportunities for spontaneous social arrangements. However, others felt this environment provided a valuable source of friends with whom the child shared similar experiences and felt comfortable with.

Getting out and about in the wider community is an essential aspect to achieving inclusion. However, many parents found managing both the disabled child and equipment on public transport and in supermarkets, etc. prohibitively difficult without help from other people. These difficulties were compounded by poor planning and design of buildings, which often prevented safe and easy access.

Participation in a variety of mainstream leisure activities is another important means of allowing children with disabilities to be part of their communities. To enable them to join in successfully, a great deal of extra effort is required from both parents and organisers, including creative thinking and forward planning. Public leisure facilities and restaurants with good disabled access and child-friendly environments provide the best locations for whole-family activities and outings, which have benefits for all. Family holidays, however, tended to be particularly problematic and unrelaxing due to the lack of familiar equipment and facilities, and difficulties in finding suitable accommodation.

CHAPTER 5

Taking on the world

Inclusion is a two-way process. Previous chapters have demonstrated the importance parents attach to their children not being excluded from the ordinary, everyday world, even though they need special kinds of help, and the efforts parents make to get their children included.

However, the success of inclusion rests as much on the attitudes of others – family, friends, neighbours, colleagues, the wider public – towards both child and family. The frequent excluding responses of society as a whole, and of individuals, can cause parents immediate pain and considerable concern for the future as well. While not all children notice stares and comments, either because they are too young or because their disability precludes understanding, their parents and other family members are aware, and upset as well. Insensitive behaviour by others can make siblings, parents and other family members reluctant to participate in activities with the disabled child.

Parents realise that, if attitudes do not alter, life in the community will be very difficult for their children as they grow up. As the length and detail of their answers indicate, this complex issue is a highly important one for parents.

FAMILY AND FRIENDS

Here I am trying to integrate him into society and my own family don't take him home to tea!

Social networks make a positive and vitally important contribution to the quality of life. The first step to including disabled children and their parents in normal social relations is for relatives and friends to recognise the child's – and the family's – special needs, and to respond with sensitivity and support.

THE EXTENDED FAMILY

Inclusion starts at home with being accepted and included in the extended family. It is clear from the research that many parents find that this fundamental process is fraught with difficulties. Even though many parents spoke positively of the welcome and understanding they and their disabled child had received, the number of comments on problems encountered within the extended family show that inclusion, even at this basic level, is still far from usual. Parents feel that learning about and coming to terms with a child's disability is a continuing process for the extended family.

Where parents comment very positively on the love and support they receive from their family, and from friends, they often qualify this by remarking how lucky they are. Parents also acknowledge how difficult it can be for their own parents and other family members to cope with the situation:

Our parents had the same feelings as us [when John was born with severe disabilities]. *They didn't know what to do for the best because obviously we are their children. I suppose they wanted to cuddle us, in a way, take care of us and take care of John. They were always there for us.*

They were very upset, it was the first grandchild on both sides, so it was very hard for them all, really very hard.

My dad really thought it was a bad move for me to adopt a child with Down's Syndrome because his impression of Down's was sitting in a corner dribbling, not really participating, not having a place in society. He was supportive but he was very, very wary. I don't think he knew quite how to cope. But now they twist him round their little finger and he's fine. There's no problem at all.

Lack of understanding about a child's delayed development or unusual behaviour creates rifts within families. Sometimes parents commented that their extended family does not appear even to try to understand and this causes great distress:

*We don't see my husband's mum, [we had] a few arguments
there, you know – 'You should be potty-training by now. When
Roy was his age he was potty-trained.' She doesn't understand.
She doesn't seek to understand.*

*My mother-in-law doesn't understand about autism at all. I'm sure
she thinks she will grow out of it completely, it's a matter of
behaviour management and if I were firmer with Christina, then
she would snap out of this and start behaving normally.*

Some families find that time, and more information, lead to
greater understanding and acceptance. Others fail to get their families to discuss the issue openly:

*The family were initially very concerned, but very confused at
what was actually wrong with John. But the more you tell them
and the more they understand about it, the easier it gets.*

*They've learnt from Jack. My mum says she has and my mother-
in-law says she's really pleased because if she sees a child with
Down's Syndrome now, she has no embarrassment. She goes up
and says hello to the child, and talks to the person and says, 'I've
got a grandson and he's got Down's Syndrome,' which is lovely
because she's actually facing up to it beautifully now.*

Family and friends often express negative attitudes towards the
child's achievements, and these contrast painfully with the positive
stance of parents themselves and of some professionals involved with
the child. Negative attitudes often stem from lack of experience of special needs and from measuring children against non-disabled peers.
The more pessimistic and negative concepts of disability prevalent
until relatively recently are another important factor, especially with
people from older generations:

*My grandma, she's seventy-five. You know what the stigma was
with special needs years ago. She always feels very sorry for him,
he can't do this, he can't do that, what kind of life will he live? And
we don't want to hear that. We don't need pity. We think: look
what he's doing! My grandma doesn't see half of what he's doing.*

I think my mother almost feels it's a bit of a social stigma. She loves Georgia, but occasionally she says things and I think she's not comfortable. She says, 'Is she still dribbling so much?' as though it's the public things [she worries about]*, and maybe comments when she was out that people were looking at her.*

Even when the extended family loves and welcomes a child with disabilities, parents still experience a lack of realistic understanding of the difficulties that the disability imposes on other children in the family and on themselves. As a result, offers of helpful, practical support are not forthcoming:

My mother, she's very proud, going round and telling everyone how she's got a handicapped granddaughter, but she does nothing for us, she just doesn't help at all. We could do with more support from my mother. I don't think she knows how hard it is, I don't think she realises.

The family said the right words, like, 'We'll all help.' But that's easy to say ... Everybody wants to see Chloe, all the family. On the practical side, though, the offers aren't there to look after her. They all want to see her and have their cuddles, but practical help is just not there.

Families find it easier to accept children who are still small enough to be treated as babies, or who can engage socially or who have no behavioural problems. This means that inclusion – even at the basic family level – can be very difficult to achieve for a child whose disabilities become more obvious as he or she grows older, or who behaves in an unusual way or cannot make good social contact:

The family, they absolutely fell in love with her as soon as they saw her. When babies like that are first born, there is no deformity, she's just another baby, you treat them as such. Well, I found we all did.

With friends and relatives, everyone knows John and accepts him. I suppose it helps because he hasn't got any behavioural problems at all, no screaming or shouting or tantrums.

Treating the disabled child quite differently from his or her siblings can make family relationships very awkward:

My mother will come in and she'll just ignore Catherine. It's very hurtful. It's very embarrassing as she's all over Jane and ignores Catherine in front of a whole lot of people.

My sister-in-law invited Sean [younger brother] to play and she hadn't invited Aidan. I was really annoyed, really upset, particularly because she left him crying on the pavement.

FRIENDS

You cannot choose your family but you can choose your friends, and friends can be a very important source of support and inclusion, supplementing – sometimes replacing – the family:

We unintentionally select friends who are easy-going, who have a household where things are less formal and Mark is allowed to rattle round.

We've lost a few friends – I suppose they can't cope with Laura's disability – so we don't see them any more.

Supportive social networks of family and friends provide the same things as all good personal relationships: understanding, support, relaxation, enjoyment and a sense of shared interests. Much of this depends on friends being aware of needs and responding appropriately without making many demands on the parents. Sometimes this comes naturally, sometimes it stems from previous experience with special needs. People who try to understand are highly valued:

My best friend's very good. She's always worked with special needs children and so she absolutely adores Lee and we go round there quite a lot.

I made a new friend and she's got a little boy [without special needs] who's actually one of Harry's best friends. She's been great and she's really involved with Harry. She understands and she wants to understand.

Some parents find their closest friends among other families with a disabled child. This can be because needs and stresses are accepted without having to be explained, and the parents can just get on with being friends, or because the situation can be discussed with people who really understand. Common experience does not guarantee instant friendship – just as with the disabled child, social networks may have to be developed until genuine friendship is found:

I suppose most of my friends, really, have got children with special needs.

I have a friend up the road who has a daughter who goes to [special school] *and it's a real help to me to talk to her about everything, everyday problems with having handicapped children, because they understand completely. You don't have to explain, the empathy is immediately there and you can suggest practical solutions and also get things a bit more into perspective by talking, things that seem insurmountable. And sometimes, things go wrong and you know they've been through the same things, and it's quite a help. But you want to choose the people you want to talk to about it.*

Friends in tune with a family's needs can make taking part in social life much easier and simpler:

If we go out to friends and they know that John has to be held or carried round all the time, they say, 'Don't worry, we'll all just take turns.' The minute you put him on the floor, he starts creating. It isn't really a problem because everyone wants to hold him anyway, so he's quite happy.

I'm most at ease in social situations with other people I know because they know everything, they know what's happened and they know Lottie. You go and say, 'Isn't she walking well now? Isn't she doing well?' and it's lovely because they make a big fuss of her.

Friends who do not have children with special needs often lack awareness and understanding. Some parents acknowledge that the biggest divide is between themselves and friends who do not have any children – something that is also true for many parents of non-disabled children. Friends' responses to the disabled child, or to the family as a whole, can also be hurtful:

Friends, they haven't got a clue, basically. They'd say, 'You look tired. It's hard work being a mum, isn't it?' And their kids are running around, getting themselves dressed, they're potty-trained, the works. Until you're actually involved with something like this ... I hadn't a clue, I must admit.

I find that friends that haven't got children with special needs don't seem to realise, they don't seem to notice anything. They just still think of her as a baby and they often tend to ignore her as well.

The obvious solution might be to explain the situation to these friends so that they come to understand the stresses and strains parents experience, and learn suitable ways to behave with the child. However, many parents commented that constantly having to explain about their child, in both private and public situations, can be exhausting and intrusive – and is certainly not expected in normal parenting. It seems to turn them into 'professional' special needs parents and isolates them from other families:

Maybe you're out in a social situation and I don't want to be talking about Lottie in that situation, I want to forget and get on with what I'm doing.

Sometimes I go into details, but other times I just say, 'Well, you know, special needs, he's disabled, that's why he's so floppy.' That sort of kills the conversation. People find that really off-putting.

Having a child with disabilities often leads to changed values and perspectives. These in turn can often make families feel isolated from their original social circle and from parents of non-disabled children:

At [her older brother's] school, I tend to think, 'These parents, they think they've got problems!'. You know, you overhear some of their conversations. It's very hard to be sympathetic. I find that quite isolating.

Since I've had Harry, I've realised what is important, getting my priorities into some sort of perspective. What really annoys me is when I see people, for instance in supermarkets, smacking their kids or saying, 'Stand still, shut up!' and I think, well, they should feel lucky that their child can walk or talk, or whatever.

A typical reaction is to minimise difficulties. Kindly but unsuitable overprotectiveness or leniency are not always the most appropriate response when parents want their child to be treated more like his or her peers:

The trouble with a lot of my friends is they were very emotionally upset when he was born ... they don't even like me talking about Jack. They say, 'He's all right, there's not a lot wrong with him.' They're not facing up to looking at him from a different view. For the first six months after he was born, I think I've never been so lonely in all my life. I never knew what loneliness was until that happened. I was so grateful that everybody cared so much, they did care, they just didn't understand.

Where we lived, all the people were so nice to Joseph. But in the summer, people used to leave their doors open and he just used to walk in, sit on people's sofas and wait. He knew what he'd get from each house, an ice cream from someone, crisps, an apple, and he'd do the rounds. I'd say to them, 'Please don't do that, he'll come in your house all the time and if you don't stop it now, he'll still be doing it when he's thirteen.' Their attitude was, 'Oh, don't worry. Your mum's an old moaner, isn't she? Come in.' You know, being kind.

They were so nervous of her because she was in pain, they did anything to avoid any sort of social discomfort like being told off. She was just allowed to queen it over everybody, and then come home like that and [we had to] get her back to normal.

It can be painful to see other children making progress and reaching milestones that your own child will find very hard, if not impossible:

One of my best friends, she had a little boy two weeks before me. That was fine to start with, but when I went to see her when Lee was about eight months old, I couldn't go again. When I saw this other little boy, how far forward he is [compared with] Lee, I just couldn't handle it and I haven't really seen her [since].

Some people find that friends and friends' children isolate the child with disabilities. It can be hard to know how best to handle this. Many parents say how hard they work to make a success of social relationships and to help other people to include their disabled child in a positive way:

Somebody invited us to [their party] *and we did go for an hour. During that hour their child took the other children upstairs out of Stephanie's way, and the parents were so busy with the food and everything else that they didn't notice that Stephanie was by herself. So there was an effort to include her, but it wasn't done with a clear eye on what was happening. She actually said later, 'Why did they keep going away?'.*

He won't go to sleep unless he's [at home] *and if it's parties, we go for an hour and then come home. If it's something during the day, we take it in turns. One of us has a drink and tries to enjoy themselves, and the other takes responsibility for Jack. We've got good friends and I don't want our friends to be relieved when we walk out of the room. As much as they love us, I think you've always got to be aware of other people.*

All this effort is often at the expense of parents' own enjoyment and friendships, for which parents often blame themselves. But there is a limit to how emotionally or physically resourceful any parent can be:

I don't include myself. Things like parties, I don't think people even notice that I'm holding her. No one ever offers to take over. Basically it's my fault. I don't like to ask, I just sit there going, 'Oh, God, they won't invite me any more if they think they're going to have to do the work.'

PUBLIC ATTITUDES

Now that the vast majority of children and young people with disabilities live at home with their families, they are out and about in public more than in the past. Parents were asked how the attitudes of the public help or hinder inclusion and again there was a lot to say. It is clear that public attitudes mean that going out and about with a disabled child is very different than with a non-disabled child. Families feel less welcome and hence sometimes more diffident about venturing out.

HAVING TO EXPLAIN

Having a child throws every parent into a world of comparisons. From pregnancy onwards all sorts of people are interested and comparisons are eagerly made: 'How much does she weigh? Has he got his first tooth yet? Can she walk? Is he talking? What school is she going to?'. In private and in public, parents quite naturally look at other children and compare their appearance, size, abilities, even their clothes, toys and equipment. It is rather like being part of a large club where all the members have similar interests.

However, when a child has special needs, comparisons become a minefield, and parents find themselves having to explain why their large child won't get out of his buggy and walk up the steps, or why their angelic-looking girl is behaving so badly and they aren't doing anything to stop her. Having to explain, perhaps to someone different, every time you step outside your house becomes very burdensome:

You have to explain, that's the thing, you have to have the explanations each time. I'd have to say she can't do the things you'd expect, she can't talk and she wouldn't understand the things they were asking her. I don't want to have to be doing that each time.

Some people seem to be intrusively interested and they've got no idea about what the problems are, and they keep asking questions – 'Can she do this and is she doing this? Oh, but medical science is discovering...'. And I find it really difficult to be civil.

It would be nice if the public were aware that there are children who are not normal and accept those children for what they are, not what you expect them to be.

Some people make obviously insensitive remarks. But other quite ordinary and well-meaning conversations can also be very difficult to cope with. Parents can come to dread other people being interested, not least because they do not always feel in the mood to handle questions and explanations:

A woman said to me, 'Oh, what a lovely baby. How old is he?'. And I said, 'He's about one and a half,' and she said, 'Really? I thought he was only six months.' And she gave me such a weird look. People think you're mad when you say he's that age when he's still acting like a six-months-old baby.

She doesn't make the normal responses and people say, 'Hello, and how are you, and what's your name?', and she just gives them a big smile. And then they look at me as if for some sort of explanation and I say, 'Well, no, she can't talk.' They are not being horrible and they are obviously attracted because she's a lovely-looking little girl, and I appreciate that, but you think, 'Oh, God, they're going to talk to her.'

Parents develop a variety of strategies to cope with these situations:

Sometimes I will actually explain and another time I'll find I'm lying. I don't think I'd be the only person who's ever lied about their child's age with a special needs child.

I can't be bothered. They're nothing to me, it's not worth it. I don't get upset about it. If you carry him and go into a shop, they say, 'Is he tired of shopping?'. I just say, 'No'. It's only worth explaining when those people are going to have more contact with him because half the time you're just embarrassed. What's the point of explaining? All you're going to achieve is embarrassing people.

On days when they can 'take on the whole world', parents believe in the value of educating people about disability. On occasions, this can lead to an improvement in how their child is treated:

I try to educate them in as gentle a way as possible. I don't get angry because they don't know any different and perhaps it could have been me. I don't knock them for not knowing, but I do try to educate them. It's my own little campaign.

A cashier actually told Christina to shut up and stop making that dreadful noise, and I said, 'Don't you dare speak to my daughter like that!' and I explained to her, and of course she was acutely embarrassed. But she won't do it to anybody else, that's for sure.

Parents of younger children can sometimes escape having to explain because the disability does not seem very apparent and other people assume that their children are still babies. But they anticipate problems later:

People don't see the disability at the moment. They just think he's a little baby. If anyone is looking, they say, 'Oh, he is a quiet little boy,' because he is quite quiet often.

When children are very young, [the disability] is not noticeable – you don't stand out because she's in a pushchair. But when they start to grow up, that's when it becomes more apparent. Because you've got a much bigger child who is maybe immobile, the handicap becomes more obvious. Even very small things become more apparent. In an older person, your expectation of their ability is more.

There is no single solution to the problem of having to explain and parents use different approaches on different days, depending on how strong or vulnerable they are feeling. Some wish people would not intrude at all, others welcome a bit of honesty:

Sometimes, I've approached people and said, 'She is handicapped,' because I know they're wanting to ask, but they won't ... I don't mind telling them. I don't like it when they just stare and stare, but I usually tell people what's wrong with her and we usually end up chatting, and that breaks the ice. I wish a lot more people would just come out with, 'What's wrong with her?' instead of just staring and wondering.

PUBLIC RESPONSES

Many parents have a horror story to tell about an incident. The most extreme demonstrate how difficult it can be to act and feel like an ordinary family going about their everyday activities:

I've had three separate people put money in her hand. They pushed it into your hand and you're so stunned, you don't have time to react. One of them said, 'That's for your crippled child.' I go through a range of reactions, usually about two hours later. It is just awful. I'm very angry. I understand that they're doing it from a motivation that cares, but it is so inappropriate, it's so hurtful.

Being stared at is a frequent experience. Some children are not aware of what is happening, either because they are too young or because of their intellectual disabilities, but parents and other adults certainly notice:

We would be walking around town and people just stare, and it's so blatant. Adults, even after you've walked past them, they actually turn round and keep staring. People seem to think we can't see them – they're staring at Catherine, obviously thinking she's not aware that they're looking at her.

You will get some odd looks, but I've really past bothering. But I think with a younger mother, this being her first or second child, this would be a really big problem to face.

Families respond in a variety of ways:

I ignore them and try not to let it affect me at all.

I'm sometimes quite embarrassed because of people's attitudes. I think it's a particularly English thing to stare and I'm only just beginning to notice that people stare at you. You end up walking along not meeting people's eyes, not looking where they're looking.

I used to get really angry, you know – 'Do you want a photo?!' – and now I don't really take much notice.

On occasions, comments are made about the child. This often happens when a child does not have any apparent disability and is not behaving appropriately for his or her age and size:

He doesn't look different. When you see a Down's child you think, 'Oh, this child's got problems.' When you've got an autistic child behaving badly, or what seems to be badly, all you get are comments that he is obviously a spoilt little brat. People would say, and out loudly so that you could hear, 'If that were my child, I'd give him a good whack.' And depending on what mood I was in that day, I would come home and have a good cry about it, or I'd turn round and be rude to them.

Now he's not in his splints during the day, people don't stare so much because his legs literally used to stick straight out and people would make comments about that. But now people wonder why a child that size is in a pushchair ... People are very reluctant to help you down steps with a double buggy because you've got this child that looks too old to be in it. And they actually say, 'It would be a lot easier if your child got out,' and you have to say, 'Well, he can't because he's got arthritis.'

It is usually mothers who have the main responsibility for child care and so they have little choice about taking their child out in public. Many feel they just have to get used to stares or comments and some do not consider this reaction hostile or rude. But sometimes, well-intentioned behaviour, like well-intentioned questions, can feel excluding:

Maybe they're just looking because he's a child. We all look at children.

We get stares, and some of the stares are, 'Isn't she lovely?' and some of them are, 'I wonder if there's something wrong with her.'

It's a very common reaction for parents to tell their children, 'Be careful of the baby' or 'the little one'. It's not that they're putting you down, it's very obvious they're saying it because he has special needs. It's not because he's little, he's bigger than their children often in size, but that's the only way they can handle his inability to move in the same way, his inability to talk. It is an exclusion because it's not really wanting to see that this is a child that has its needs like any other, that has its will and its tantrums, and is not to be belittled.

Noticeable equipment such as wheelchairs, large pushchairs, unusual seating and so on, draw attention to children and can lead to staring and comments:

When Chloe is in her normal buggy, I don't think people tend to notice. When she is in her wheelchair, most people don't say anything, they just tend to stare, and children are terrible. Lots of people come up and say, 'That's a great buggy,' and I tend to be really horrible and say, 'It's not a buggy, it's a wheelchair.' Just, you know, leave me alone, I'm just trying to be normal and go shopping normally. I think most people are trying to be kind, but...

We had problems when we were given a really ugly chair for Joanne. It was quite old and the appearance was gross. It looked as though it had typically come from a hospital and we found all the children were looking at it and associating Joanne in a bad way with the chair, and they wouldn't go near her. And they said, 'What's wrong with her?'.

The crucial questions for parents are why other people respond in this way and what sort of response they would ideally like. While ignorance is seen as the prime cause of other people's lack of interest and even hostility, views differ about the most helpful, positive responses. What suits one family might not suit another; in any case, much depends on the day-to-day situation. Some parents welcome questions to 'clear the air' and have no difficulty in answering; others dislike what they feel to be intrusive questioning. Some think that it is inevitable that their child will be stared at, just as they look at other children for all sorts of reasons including finding them charming and delightful, and that looking is not always because of ignorant curiosity and hostility. Some parents accept that using a wheelchair or other uncommon equipment is bound to attract attention, while in the experience of others, obtrusive equipment simply underlines the differences and creates a barrier between their child and other people:

I think it's people not knowing, it's their ignorance, they are scared, they don't know how to respond.

I find people switch off because they don't really want to know. I can't blame them for that, but I think it's sad because if they knew, they wouldn't fear.

There isn't enough made known about children with any form of special needs. On television, for example, you never see any child with any problems at all.

DEVELOPING SELF-ESTEEM

Many parents talked about ways of building their child's self-esteem to help him or her to cope with the outside world and to ensure that people respond to the child as positively as possible. Giving a lead, both to the child and to others, is of key importance:

I've always tried very much to behave towards Aidan as if he were normal because I really feel that people take cues from you. And if I outwardly behave as if he were different, then they would take that [cue] from me.

I think without a very positive attitude, and even a pushy attitude, by the parents, a child like Tim would get very little out of other people. There's always a wariness in other people's approach to Tim, they don't know how to respond to him. When we meet other people and they talk to us, I always include Tim in the conversation. I always talk to him as I would any other person, and that reassures people that he understands and he's responsive.

Appearance is an important factor, irrespective of whether the child is aware of how he or she looks, and can determine other people's responses:

I'm very conscious of how she looks, she has to look just so, she has to have her hair brushed and combed and nice dresses on, and I won't have her going out looking a mess. Whereas with my other two, it doesn't matter so much with them. Because you know when they look messy, they look lovely still. But Lottie – I feel it's important how she looks ... I think [looking nice] is good for self-esteem and people do react to appearances. You just do.

I'd like them to have ordinary friends because – not being exactly a young mother – when they get to the time when they want to dress fashionably, they're going to have friends they can go with who can give them an idea of the sort of thing you should be wearing. I hate seeing these Down's children in their pop socks, just looking like all their clothes have been gathered from the local jumble sales. They're not dressed in a smart and modern way.

As children grow, they become more aware of their disability and this affects their self-image:

He knows he's got arthritis and he knows he does his exercises twice a night, and he knows he has his Brufen and his steroids, but that's as far as it goes. He doesn't think of himself as a disabled child. Not yet. We don't think of him as that disabled sometimes, either. Five is about when they become a bit more aware of the problem.

Now when he sees children younger than him walking, one or two years old, he just watches their feet all the time as though to say, 'God, how are they doing that?'. He doesn't look at their faces any more, he just looks at their feet all the time.

At the [mainstream] *school, he didn't see himself as particularly different. The time came when he couldn't cope there and we moved him to his special school. He realised he was in a school where there were very disabled children, he had ended up among disability and he'd never really looked at disability before. It's probably a good thing that it didn't hit him until about eleven and a half because he was actually able to hold an image of himself which wasn't particularly a disabled image. It's given him a very different view of himself and the world, and I think now he's very reluctant to go into the outside world and join in other activities, and the main reason is that he gets teased.*

Parents feel that they need to be aware of how their children are reacting to the responses of other people and how their own self-image is evolving:

Children can say things that are cruel and I hope as Georgia gets older she'll understand. She's in a very protected environment at the moment. Obviously, she's going to encounter people being unkind and our approach is that the more people she mixes with earlier, the wider her circle of experience and friends will be. And, hopefully, when she reaches the unpleasant situation that inevitably she will, she'll be able to have some sort of balance with the satisfaction and security from all the other people that she knows, to put it into some sort of perspective.

While he's on top of things, he's happy and lively, but I think underneath there's just such a deep sadness about their condition that they can go down really, really quickly, and that affects the family.

Extending experiences, giving children opportunities to make good

friends and to find activities that they enjoy, and at which they can perhaps excel, all help to build self-esteem:

> You just accept [the disability], *just get on with it, because there
> are things he can do better than other children, like swim on his
> own without armbands. And he loves it, he'd swim under water
> and jump off the side, he absolutely loves it. If he hadn't had this
> chronic illness, he probably wouldn't be doing that.*

EXTENDING PUBLIC AWARENESS

Many parents themselves knew nothing about disability before it
became part of their immediate family and can excuse other people's
inappropriate responses by saying that they might have done the same
before having their child. Some feel that people's awareness has
increased a great deal since they were children because greater educational integration means that children, if not adults, are used to having
others with special needs around them:

> *People are so quick to judge. I mean, I've done it myself when I
> was a single person. You see a child behaving abysmally in a
> supermarket and you think, 'My goodness, she's obviously got no
> control over that child,' or, 'What a spoilt little brat'. Now I think,
> 'Well, maybe they've got some problems'. Now I will stop and
> say, 'Can I help you with anything?'.*

However, some parents find it hard to educate even the people
closest to them about their child's disability and special needs:

> *My own mother tries to understand but hasn't quite got a grasp
> on it, even after eight years, so they're* [the public] *not likely to get
> much more of a grasp on it.*

Some parents believe that education about disability should be part
of the school curriculum. Others believe that greater integration at
school and in outside activities would help, but if it is to be successful,
and thoroughly welcomed by everyone involved, it must be well
planned and provide positive outcomes for both disabled and non-disabled children. Public awareness could also be improved by the media
– for instance, by including children with special needs more generally
in mainstream television programmes and advertisements:

I do really feel that to have children with special needs in mainstream schools is a great help to other children.

It should be involved in curriculums at school, special needs. Even if children don't have special needs at their school, they should still be aware of what problems you can have and why they have them.

Why do they always put programmes about disability on t.v. late at night so children can't see them, but also adults may not bother? Now we make a point of watching these things, but I have to say we didn't before. But if they were on at peak viewing we might have watched.

LOOKING AHEAD

IMMEDIATE HOPES AND ASPIRATIONS

In the short term, parents' aspirations for their children are largely practical. For younger children, they want to extend the positive examples of inclusion that they have already enjoyed to give them more fulfilling and rounded experiences:

I'd like him to be able to be integrated, to be more with other children. The integrated playscheme was great and it does work for both sets of children. I would like to see more of that.

[At the integrated playgroup] they're going to include her in absolutely everything – she's going to paint, she's going to play in the sandpit, go in the ball-pool, soft playroom, everything.

I'd like him to be able to do something one afternoon after school, to be dropped off somewhere. He couldn't go to a gym club or a dance club or karate, but there's bound to be something he could join.

For more severely disabled children, attending special school is seen as a positive step towards achieving their potential. Being part of a community of school children represents an important step forward:

We're looking forward to when he can go to school, you know, special school. I think that will be another good step for him because we're doing a lot for him, but there'd be a stage where he must be with other people, to be in a school environment.

I'd like to see him, when he does go to school, where he is in a class and he is taking part, and I can see him enjoy it, actually laughing because he is enjoying it. It's very hard for John to express his feelings or show he is enjoying something.

Parents of older children are aware of their growing desire for independence and of the support they need to achieve as much as possible. They also realise that the process is two-way – the outside world must adapt its attitudes:

He needs his independence. I think more than anything else he needs good self-esteem. These teenage years are very hard.

Paul is so sort of independent and does so want to do his own thing. He so wants to be ordinary like everyone else.

Parents are aware that their child will have to learn to cope with the outside world:

She's only four, but it's a rough old world out there, so it's a little bit of gentle exposure in controlled environments ... You try to protect them in the environment they're in and try and guide them towards certain areas where you think they're going to meet civilised people – but the world isn't full of civilised people.

In some cases, equipment, and the finance to provide it, are seen as the key to their child's inclusion in the ordinary community:

He's on a par intellectually and educationally with his able-bodied speaking peers, it's only the lack of equipment to facilitate his communicating, his writing. I'm not happy with my child speaking a kind of pidgin English through basic symbols when there is a capacity for him to speak in his own words, using whatever words he's picked up colloquially through his natural development.

THE LONG-TERM VIEW

Some parents have clear ideas about their child's future and how they want him or her to be included in the community:

My hope for Jack is that when he's an adult, he can walk into a pub on his own, order a pint of beer, speak clearly and be able to converse clearly with those around him so that regardless of the depth of the conversation, they won't have to work hard to understand him and he will just be accepted as, 'Well, that's Jack, a regular.'

We'd like her to have as much education as possible, whether she stays in special school or goes to mainstream school, or has a combination of the two. Clearly, if she can get a good education, that's the best way for her to cope when she's an adult. If she can get any form of professional qualification – that's what will make her independent.

Other parents are less clear about the route to inclusion, but stress that their aim is for a happy and useful life:

You hope they will have a happy life with all the friendships, love, everything else that a normal person would have, like a job.

I would really like him to lead a normal life, I mean if he is in a wheelchair, then as normal a life as possible. And to make things as easy for him as possible and for him to enjoy life thoroughly.

A common concern among all the parents able to look so far ahead is that young adults should be helped to develop as much self-esteem and independence as possible, but in a safe and caring environment appropriate to their needs, and perhaps alongside other people with special needs:

I'm inclined to think, 'Oh, I'll look after Mark,' because he's mine, but we've got to look at ways to get him out of our clutches. That would be normal if he didn't have special needs and it's not less so because he has special needs. I imagine in my wildest dreams that he'd live in a small unit with other adults with special needs who were supervised, akin to a family house. That's my dream, that he lives away from us, but near enough to visit, just as I hope I'll be able to see my other children and enjoy birthdays, Christmas, holidays with them, but that he is afforded the autonomy of living away from home.

I'd ideally like her to have some sort of simple job, even if it is only washing up or something. I don't like to think of her spending the rest of her life marking time and not doing anything. I'd like her to feel that she's being productive – even if she isn't being particularly productive – but just to have some sort of self-esteem. But where she's going to get it, I don't know.

Parents are quite aware of the kind of society in which all children grow up, and are realistic about opportunities for disabled and non-disabled people alike:

He's Jack first, he's got to learn that, Jack first and Down's Syndrome comes second, and some things they won't be included in, much as it hurts – but life's like that, isn't it? And I don't want him to lay it all on one thing.

If he wants a girlfriend, I'd like him to be able to get one – I mean, not everyone's able to get one anyway, whether they're able-bodied or not. He should be able to have the chance of a job, if everyone else has got the chance of a job. If there are no jobs about, that's fair enough. But he shouldn't be rejected just because he's got problems physically.

For other parents, inclusion means their child with disabilities continuing to live at home with the family, but with sufficient support to make this practicable:

Long-term, we hope to keep him with us always, or we will do if we possibly can, but to do that we also understand that we will need the backup of the social services or we just wouldn't be able to do it on our own. When he gets to fifteen or sixteen, he's going to be a big boy and a lot of hard work. We really will need all the help we can get for him to stay with us.

I don't want her to have to leave home, but I want her not to be at home 24 hours a day because she'll need educating for life. And Lottie needs all the stimulation she can get, she can't get out and get stimulation, she's got to have it brought to her. If she doesn't have that, she'll go into a decline, the same as anyone would who was shut up in a room and didn't have anything to do. It's like being in prison – even in prison people get educated.

Some parents feel very unsure about what the future holds for their child, or cannot even contemplate it. All that is clear is that their child's future, and their family's, will be very different from other families where the children do not have special needs:

> *I haven't got a clue, I just haven't got a clue. I don't know what direction we're going into. I see it a bit bleak in the future because nobody can tell me what he'll be like.*

> *Long term, I can't bear to think about. I never, ever think about the future.*

> *The only way I can cope is by thinking about tomorrow and next week. Certainly, ten years ahead I can't bear to think of.*

Parents' 'wildest dreams' for their children's future are in no sense wild, and are tempered by awareness of economic realities and the limited amount of suitable provision available. Some parents worry about what will happen when their child reaches the age of nineteen and no longer enjoys the social protection and services provided by legislation applying to children. The present is hard work, with a struggle to obtain the support that they and their child need, and they foresee a lifetime of struggle, whether or not their child is included in the community:

> *I'm scared of what happens when the respite [care] goes, because it will go for her when she's nineteen.*

> *I'd like to see him actively involved in the wider community because there's no reason why, if he wants to, that he shouldn't, other than that the facilities aren't made available. I'm very wary that these facilities might not be available for whatever reason – cost, maybe.*

> *The future's so bleak, the future after school is abysmal. We're just looking into it at the moment, what's going to happen at nineteen plus. Because Lottie will be at school till she's nineteen – and what happens then? The children, they're back to mum and dad.*

SUMMARY

Good personal relationships made a great difference to how well supported the family felt and the range of inclusive social opportunities they and their child had access to. However, even within the extended family, or with friends, inclusion was not necessarily automatic or easy to achieve due to lack of awareness and experience of disability. All families seemed to value their links with others in a similar situation and some parents found they had limited their social network to families like this.

The general public responded to families with a disabled child in a variety of ways, from supportive to downright offensive. Public responses that could be construed as hostile were upsetting and prevented families from feeling comfortably anonymous as they went about their everyday business in public. Such attitudes could also impact on the self-esteem of the child, especially as he or she grew towards greater independence.

Worries about the future were extremely stressful and isolating for families with children with disabilities. Much of the provision talked about in this report, including respite care, changes or stops when the child reaches nineteen, and many families were worried that horizons for their child and themselves actually narrowed, rather than widened, as the young person moved towards adulthood.

CHAPTER 6

Conclusion

This qualitative study of the lives and thoughts of parents of disabled children has concentrated as much on the in-depth reporting of their feelings and fears, hopes and aspirations as on recording the practical changes that would make their lives easier. Part of the value of the research lies in the opportunity it provides to comprehend the everyday reality of caring for and bringing up a child with disabilities. The hopes and joys, as well as the sadnesses, are so like those of parents of non-disabled children – yet so entirely different as well.

A small group of young people with disabilities was also consulted in the acknowledgement that the young people were likely to have different opinions, experiences and aspirations to those their parents expect them to have. The young people provided a brief insight into their lives, and their feelings of inclusion and difference. Most notable, however, were the more limited horizons to which those in their later teens, especially, could aspire, demonstrating the narrower range of choices and variety of experience available to most young disabled people.

The parents themselves provided a wealth of vivid and poignant detail showing that inclusion did happen, but often on account of enormous effort on their part. Balancing hectic therapeutic schedules with the needs of other siblings, facilitating and developing friendships for and with their child, and ensuring he or she participated fully in a range of activities, called for a great deal of resourcefulness and imaginative forward planning by parents. The physical, mental and emotional cost to families was great and parents had to look carefully at the benefits to their disabled child, to other children in the family, and to themselves, to see where their efforts were best concentrated.

It was clear that integrated schooling and leisure activities could provide enormous benefits for the disabled child, their non-disabled peers and society as a whole. However, in certain circumstances, mainstream environments were not viewed as the most appropriate solution due to a lack of understanding of, or inability to meet, the child's specific needs, or simply because it was felt to be more beneficial to the child to mix with those with whom he or she has more shared experience and may thus feel more comfortable with. Ideally, a range of mainstream and specialist environments should be available to children with disabilities so that their needs can be adequately met at every level of their day-to-day lives.

The parents had all experienced unhelpful or insensitive attitudes from members of the public, and sometimes from services designed to help them. Such behaviour makes the task of getting their child included in ordinary life even harder. All parents felt that increased public awareness of disability in all realms of society was vital in fostering understanding and acceptance.

Despite the difficulties and struggles, all the parents surveyed thought it was important that their child should have as many opportunities as possible to be included in the community, regardless of the nature or extent of his or her disability. Inclusion benefits children with special needs by offering them a full range of experiences and the chance to fulfil their potential and be treated as an equal member of society. Inclusion benefits the community by educating people about disability and the general differences between people, and by enhancing tolerance and understanding. Whatever specific services are offered, or opportunities created, to provide inclusion, they must be of the highest quality in order to ensure a positive experience.

The long-term future for families with a disabled child was a daunting and uncertain prospect which many parents could barely bring themselves to contemplate. All parents felt that good-quality support was essential to extend the opportunities for inclusion already experienced and enable their child to develop self-esteem and as much independence as possible. Paradoxically, much-needed support systems are withdrawn once the young people reach the age of nineteen, thus limiting their horizons further. It is vital to recognise that young people with disabilities do not stop learning and expanding their horizons just because formal educational provision has ceased.

RECOMMENDATIONS FOR POLICY AND PRACTICE

From the research there emerge many specific, practical recommendations for changes in policy and practice designed to bring about a greater measure of inclusion. These apply particularly to professionals: caregivers in health and social services, educationalists and related specialists. However, their underlying message – to value people with disabilities and their families as much as any other person – applies equally to each and every individual as friend, neighbour or citizen.

RESPITE CARE

The availability of good respite care underpins all the efforts families make for their disabled children living at home. Good respite care should:

- be available before the need becomes desperate;

- be offered for short and long periods, to suit family and individual needs;

- mix formal care (by trained, paid staff) with care by volunteers, as appropriate, with good training opportunities for all respite carers;

- take into account the needs of the whole family and include siblings as well as the child with disabilities.

SERVICES

Services for children with disabilities must recognise that disabled children are part of young families and take into account the needs of the whole family. Good-quality services should:

- fix appointments at convenient times;

- be accessible, with a friendly atmosphere and opportunities for play in the waiting areas;

- be provided as close to the family home as possible;

- be offered alongside services for non-disabled children;

- be provided willingly, without parents having to fight for them;

- provide transport that does not exclude other dependent children.

Professionals should:

- recollect that a child with disabilities is first and foremost a child, whose parents must have time to play and relax with him or her;

- remember that parents should have a free choice about which services they want to use without feeling that this might damage their child's future development;

- make relevant, up-to-date information easily accessible;

- minimise the amount of paperwork that parents need to complete.

LEISURE ACTIVITIES

Improved integrated facilities for children (and adults) with disabilities would enable families to participate in leisure activities together. Integrated facilities allow disabled and non-disabled children to enjoy activities and friends in common. Leisure, sporting and allied organisations should:

- provide facilities for both disabled and non-disabled children, so that the whole family can enjoy time out together;

- adopt a creative approach to play and recreation, for example, by providing play equipment suitable for disabled children and swimming pools with a range of temperatures;

- implement policies for involving children with disabilities as a matter of course, so that this no longer depends on the willingness of particular individuals;

- foster a more sympathetic understanding of disability among staff through staff training programmes;

- ensure that facilities advertised as suitable for people with disabilities really are so, and in particular are appropriate for disabled children.

Support groups for siblings of disabled children allow them to meet other children in similar circumstances, decrease their sense of isolation and enable them to enjoy activities they cannot take part in when their disabled sibling is present.

FRIENDSHIPS

Providing opportunities for real friendships to develop will minimise exclusion and allow children to grow in independence and autonomy. The following recommendations are aimed primarily at providers of after-school and holiday play and activities, as well as leisure organisations. Many parents recognised these steps as the way forward and were already doing these things informally. However, their efforts need to be supported in a formal capacity. Friendships can be fostered by:

- providing well thought out play and social opportunities with a mixture of integrated and non-integrated activities;

- sensitive supervision and handling of play and other activities;

- forward planning to enable children with disabilities to meet and socialise with their friends;

- arranging more flexible school transport so as to maximise after-school socialising.

THE COMMUNITY ENVIRONMENT

Planners should provide safe, suitable and welcoming environments for people with disabilities as a crucial factor of inclusion. Planners in both the public and private sectors, as well as those responsible for managing shops and other amenities, should:

- ensure real ease of access (not token gestures) for people in wheelchairs and pushchairs to shops, public buildings, etc.;

- carry out regular disability audits on public places;

- provide full information about places with disabled access;

- provide more staff to help carers with a disabled child or children;

- manage disabled parking facilities so that the system works effectively.

THE SOCIAL NETWORK

Good personal and family relationships make an enormous difference to the functioning of families with disabled children. Individual attitudes are the key among families and friends. Social attitudes are also of great importance. Targets for change include addressing the following areas:

- negative attitudes to disability, especially among older generations;

- inconsistent, spoiling treatment of a child with disabilities by friends and the extended family – parents will probably have their own guidelines, which should be followed;

- greater understanding to overcome the almost inevitable gap in experience between friends with and without children with disabilities;

- lack of practical and moral support that leaves parents and siblings socially isolated.

These issues could be influenced significantly by:

- using the education system to increase awareness and understanding of disability;

- improving images of disability in the media through positive, sympathetic treatment of the issues and of individuals with disabilities.

Bibliography

Appleton, P. (1995) 'Young people with a disability: Aspects of social empowerment.' C. Cloke and M. Davis (eds.) *Participation and Empowerment in Child Protection*. London: Pitman.

Association of Metropolitan Authorities (1994) *Special Children, Special Needs*. London.

Atkinson, N., Crawforth, M. (1995) *All in the Family: Siblings and Disability*. London: NCH – Action for Children.

Bennett, F., Abrahams, C. (1994) *Unequal Opportunities: Children with Disabilities and their Families Speak Out*. London: NCH – Action for Children.

Beresford, B. (1994) *Positively Parents: Caring for a Severely Disabled Child*. London: HMSO.

Beresford, B. (1995) *Expert Opinions: A National Survey of Parents Caring for a Severely Disabled Child*. Bristol: The Policy Press.

Centre for Studies on Inclusive Education (1994) 'Talking Inclusion'. An audiotape and background worksheet featuring children and young people with and without disabilities talking about learning together. London.

Clarke, P., Kofsky, H., Laurol, J. (1989) *To a Different Drumbeat: A Practical Guide to Parenting Children with Special Needs*. Stroud: Hawthorne Press.

Cowen, A., (1994) *Taking Care*. York: The Joseph Rowntree Foundation.

Dale, N. (1996) *Working with Families of Children with Special Needs: Partnership and Practice*. London: Routledge.

Exley, H. (ed.) (1984) *What It's Like to Be Me*. Friendship Press.

Geall, R., Host, N. (1991) *Sharing the Caring: Respite Care in the UK for Families with Children with Disabilities*. London: NCH – Action for Children.

Goodey, C. F. (ed.) (1991) *Living in the Real World: Families Speak Out about Down's Syndrome*. London: The Twenty One Press.

Hales, G. (1996) *Beyond Disability: Towards an Enabling Environment*. London: Sage.

Hornby, G. (1994) *Counselling in Child Disability*. London: Chapman Hall.

Lamb, B., Layzell, S. (1994) *Disabled in Britain: A World Apart*. London: Scope.

Lamb, B., Layzell, S. (1995) *Disabled in Britain: Behind Closed Doors – the Carer's Experience*. London: Scope.

Network of Parents of Children with Special Needs (1996) *Through the Maze: An Information Handbook*. Hove and Portslade Voluntary Care Services.

Network of Parents of Children with Special Needs (1996) 'Supporting Siblings of Children with Special Needs'. A report of a workshop held in Portslade, East Sussex, July 9.

Newson, E., Davies, J. (1994) 'Supporting the siblings of children with autism and related developmental disorders'. P. Mittler and M. Mittler (eds.) *Innovations in Family Support for People with Learning Disabilities*. Chorley: Brothers of Charity, Lisieux Hall.

Oswin, M. (1984, revised 1991) *They Keep Going Away: A Critical Study of Short-term Residential Care Services for Children with Learning Disabilities*. London: King Edward's Hospital Fund for London.

Swain, J., Frankelstein, V., French, S., Oliver, M. (eds.) (1993) *Disabling Barriers, Enabling Environments*. London and Milton Keynes: Sage Publications/Open University.

Weinhouse, D., Weinhouse, M. (1994) *Little Children, Big Needs: Parents Discuss Raising their Children with Exceptional Needs*. Niwot, Colorado: University Press of Colorado.

THE CHILDREN'S SOCIETY

The Children's Society is a Christian organisation which exists to work with and for children and young people, regardless of race, culture or creed.

The Children's Society runs more than 90 projects throughout England and Wales, including:

- family centres and neighbourhood groups in local communities where families are under stress, often feeling isolated and powerless to improve their lives;

- providing independent living units for young people leaving care;

- working with young people living on the street;

- offering independent guardians *ad litem* for children involved in care proceedings;

- residential and day care for children and young people with disabilities;

- helping children and young people with special needs to find new families;

- promoting the rights of children and young people.

The Children's Society is committed to raising public awareness of issues affecting children and young people and to promoting their welfare and rights in matters of public policy. The Society produces a wide range of publications, including reports, briefing papers and educational material.

For further information about the work of The Children's Society or to obtain a publications list, please contact:

The Publishing Department
The Children's Society
Edward Rudolf House
Margery Street
London WC1X 0JL

Tel. 0171-837 4299   Fax 0171-837 0211